NOVAK DJOKOVIC

THE GREATEST OF ALL TIME

NOVAK DJOKOVIC

THE GREATEST OF ALL TIME

DOMINIC BLISS

IVY PRESS

Quarto

First published in 2024 by Ivy Press,
an imprint of The Quarto Group.
One Triptych Place
London, SE1 9SH,
United Kingdom
T (0)20 7700 6700
www.Quarto.com

A catalogue record for this book is available from the British Library.

ISBN 978-0-7112-8927-7
Ebook ISBN 978-0-7112-8929-1

10 9 8 7 6 5 4 3 2 1

Design by Dave Jones

Publisher: Richard Green
Assistant Editor: Katerina Menhennet
Art Director: Paileen Currie
Production Controller: Maeve Healy and Rohana Yusof

Printed in China

This book is not endorsed by Novak Djokovic.

CONTENTS

INTRODUCTION

In years to come, sports fans will look back on the early 21st century as a golden age in men's tennis, with three champions – Roger Federer, Rafa Nadal and Novak Djokovic – dazzling us with their exploits on court. Of those three, it is Novak who shines the most brightly. He has eclipsed Federer and Nadal and, at time of writing, held a record-breaking 24 Grand Slam singles titles.

Now that Federer has retired, and Nadal has announced 2024 will be his final season, Novak's dominance seems assured. He leads in not only Grand Slam victories but also the other two metrics commonly used to measure greatness: number of tournament titles and number of weeks as world number one. What's more, the Serbian player's form suggests he has plenty more magic left to give us.

In the past, misunderstandings and PR gaffes (especially over his Covid vaccination status) have tarnished his reputation somewhat. However, if he continues to win at the highest level, some of that lost gloss will return. He is, after all, an amenable fellow, keen to please his fans and support his various charity ventures.

In this book, we examine all features of the human being behind the player: his childhood in war-torn Belgrade, his place within Serbian culture, and his myriad sponsorships and business ventures. We analyse his playing style, his fitness regime, his unorthodox diet and his embrace of alternative medicine. We look at his relationship with his wife, his kids, his controversial father, his multiple coaches, and his endless striving for more and more Grand Slam titles.

Interspersed between these personal and professional aspects of Novak's life are ten of the most important matches of his career. Starting with his first ATP title in 2006, and reliving his most glorious performances in Grand Slams and Davis Cups, we chart the crucial milestones on his journey to becoming the world-beating champion that everyone so admires today.

Meanwhile, peppered throughout the book are the most important statistics of his career on the court. Sport is often an unusual marriage of human character and mathematical statistics. We must gauge both if we are to truly understand this brilliant and sometimes enigmatic Serbian.

RIGHT: Novak with his 24th Grand Slam trophy, at the 2023 US Open.

"I will always stay in tennis in whatever shape, form or role. I feel like the love for the tennis will never fade away.

Novak Djokovic

LEFT: Signing autographs at the US Open in 2014.

YOUNG NOLE

1

LEFT: On the apartment building where Novak's grandfather, Vlada, used to live there is a mural depicting Novak's coach Jelena Genčić, Novak and his grandfather.

They say lightning never strikes the same place twice. It was this rather flawed idea that guided Novak Djokovic when he was growing up in Belgrade during the NATO bombing campaign of 1999. For 78 days straight, Novak and his family would spend nights taking refuge in a bomb shelter beneath his aunt's apartment building. In the days in between, when the bombing eased up, he would search out tennis courts to practise on with his coach Jelena Genčić.

He and Genčić would purposefully choose the sites of the most recent attacks, believing that since NATO had targeted a certain location the day before, they were unlikely to bomb it the following day. Inevitably, they were forced to play on courts with cracked concrete and, often, no nets. In a time of war, it was a risky pastime. But Novak was so dedicated to his tennis, and his coach so convinced of her young charge's future success, that they were both willing to run the gauntlet. Jelena continued the coaching even after her sister was killed by collapsing rubble.

Sometimes pupil and coach dared to practise at their local tennis club, Partizan, which was particularly risky, located as it was close to one of the city's military schools, and therefore slap-bang in a potential strike zone. Despite the threat, Novak says he felt strangely safe at his tennis club, often practising for many hours. He even took part in kids' tournaments staged on quieter days during the lengthy bombing campaign.

Childhood traumas define a person's character, shaping aspects of it well into later life. For Novak, his childhood trauma was this NATO bombing of his home city.

It was 1999, and he was just 11 years old. For the entirety of that decade, ethnic tensions had been fuelling vicious wars and insurgencies all across much of former Yugoslavia. By 1998, hostilities had moved to Kosovo, a province in the south of Yugoslavia, bordering Albania. In an attempt to bring to an end atrocities committed against ethnic

Albanians by troops under the command of Slobodan Milošević, NATO implemented a relentless aerial bombing campaign which lasted for two-and-a-half months, between March and June 1999. Unfortunately, Belgrade bore the brunt of the air strikes. Novak and his family were among the myriad Serbs who suffered because of them.

In his 2013 autobiography *Serve to Win*, Novak relives those early years. "A boy like me, growing up in Serbia, becoming a tennis champion? It was unlikely in even the best of circumstances," he wrote. "And it became ever more unlikely when the bombs started dropping."

One terrifying night, the very first of the air raids on Belgrade, will always stand out in his memory. It was the evening of March 24th, and Novak was drifting off to sleep in the family apartment, in a residential part of Belgrade called Banjica, a short distance south of the city centre. He was suddenly awoken by an ear-splitting explosion, shattering glass and air-raid sirens. "It was as though we were living inside a snow globe and someone had hurled it to the floor," he remembers.

His mother Dijana temporarily lost consciousness after slipping over and striking her head against a radiator. While his father Srdjan tried to bring her round, Novak quickly gathered together his two younger brothers, Marko, eight, and Djordje, just four.

Novak and his parents knew what they had to do. As soon as his mother had regained consciousness, all five of them scrambled down the stairs of their apartment building, and out into the dark streets of Belgrade. They needed the refuge of a bomb shelter, and the nearest one was 300 metres away, beneath the apartment building where Novak's aunt lived.

Racing down the street were his parents, with his brothers in tow. Novak was following behind, as fast as he could. Suddenly he stumbled and fell, sprawling face-first into the road.

With bombs falling all around, his calls for help couldn't be heard. "'Mama! Papa!' I cried out, but they couldn't hear me," he recalls. "I saw their forms growing smaller and dimmer, disappearing into the night."

Frightened for his life, Novak heard a deafening roar from behind him. On turning he saw the ominous triangular grey shadow of an F-117 stealth bomber appearing over the roof of his apartment building. "I watched in horror as its great metal belly opened directly above me," he wrote in his autobiography, "and two laser-guided missiles dropped out of it, taking aim at my family, my friends, my neighbourhood – everything I'd ever known. What happened next would never leave me. Even today, loud sounds fill me with fear."

The twin rockets exploded into a nearby hospital building, instantly setting it alight. "I remember the sandy, dusty, metallic smell in the air, and how the whole city seemed to glow like a ripe tangerine."

Pulling himself up off the ground, Novak spotted his parents in the distance and fled after them. Together they all crowded into the aunt's bomb shelter, along with 20 or so other families. "I didn't stop shivering for the rest of the night."

BELOW: The Djokovic family (from left to right): Dijana, Sdrjan, Djordje and Marko at the 2009 Monte-Carlo Rolex Masters.

In a recent video interview, Novak discussed his lasting memories of that night. "That is one of the most traumatic experiences and images I had in my childhood," he said in a podcast interview called "In Depth with Graham Bensinger" in 2021. "It stayed with me to this day. We were lucky, our families, that we didn't lose anybody who was very close to us. A lot of people lost very close people in their lives, and that's a different level of suffering and different level of trauma. I can't imagine the pain I'd have to bear to go through that."

For many of those scary nights in the spring of 1999, Novak and his family hid in that bomb shelter. In the evening, at around 8pm when sirens sounded the alarm for imminent attacks, they would rush down the road and join other frightened families. Novak explained how they would try to sleep, but the constant explosions would rouse them. He described the feeling of horror and helplessness. "There was nothing we could do but to sit and wait and hope and pray. It was a horrifying experience for everyone. Particularly for children. We did not realise what was happening. Why are the planes flying over our city and dropping bombs? Who does that?"

ABOVE: Many Serbians learned to carry on as normal during the bombing; these children found a new playground on a wrecked Serbian Army tank.

After a while, Novak admits he and his family became rather complacent and stoical about the danger. It was an attitude he noticed in many of his fellow Serbians. With so much death and destruction around them, eventually they grew sick of being afraid, he remembers. "Once you realise that you are truly powerless, a certain sense of freedom takes over. What will happen will happen, and there is nothing you can do to alter it."

As the bombs continued to fall, this stoicism increased. On May 22nd, Novak celebrated his 12th birthday with friends at his Partizan tennis club. He remembers how, just as everyone was singing "Happy birthday" in his honour, a NATO bomber swooped overhead. They were all so habituated to the sound that it had become mere background noise.

Years later, though, it would be obvious that Novak's world view was deeply affected by his experience in 1999. During the 2013 US Open he was asked his opinion on whether the US government should support air strikes on Syria, whose government was believed to have used chemical weapons on its own citizens.

"War is the worst thing in life for humanity," he said. "Nobody really wins. I'm totally against any kind of weapon, any kind of air strike, missile attack. I'm totally against anything that is destructive. Because I had this personal experience, I know it cannot bring any good to anybody."

Novak is a committed pacifist and, given his tumultuous early years, that's hardly surprising. He now talks of a new "philosophy of life".

Originally, he felt anger and a deep sense of injustice, all fomented by memories of that NATO bombing campaign. He claims he used that anger to fuel his success on the tennis court but, after many years, he realised the same anger was preventing him from moving on in life.

"I really don't have this emotion anymore," he said in his interview with Graham Bensinger. "I will not forget what happened, but at the same time I don't think it's good for anybody to be stuck in the emotions of hatred, anger, rage."

All Serbians were angered by the destruction of the NATO bombings, he explains. But he realised he and his compatriots needed to forgive the aggressors. "How can you be fuelled more by anything but by love?" he said. "Love is forgiveness. That's my philosophy of life. And as hard as it might be, at the end of the day, you can and you should forgive. You have to move on. If you are stuck in that emotion [of rage], what are you going to make out of your life? It's always going to hold you back, hold you down. Not just professionally but privately, emotionally."

He believes the suffering and privations experienced by him and his fellow Serbians have, ultimately, made them all stronger, more resilient. His own strength and resilience are displayed on the tennis court to this day.

Novak was born on May 22nd 1987, in Belgrade. At the time, his parents, Srdjan and Dijana, ran a restaurant in the city. Two years later, Novak's father and uncle Goran teamed up to open a second restaurant – a pizza parlour called Red Bull – in a mountain resort in the south of the country, called Kopaonik. Here they also ran a sports equipment shop. Novak's parents would split their time between Kopaonik and Belgrade, living in the mountains during the ski seasons in winter and the hiking seasons in summer, and then back in the city in spring and autumn.

During the school holidays Novak and his two brothers would stay in the mountains but during term time they would live back in Belgrade for their schooling, staying with their grandfather Vlada in his apartment. He had an enormous influence on their upbringing, according to Novak. Although he died in 2012, there's a mural of his face painted on the wall of the apartment block he used to live in, alongside a picture of Novak and Genčić.

Novak himself describes his early childhood – before the war – as "magic, especially blessed". One blessing, in particular, was when the government decided to build a tennis academy in Kopaonik, just across the street from the pizza parlour.

Had this academy not been built, would young Novak – or Nole, as his family called him – have taken up the sport? Possibly not. His parents weren't tennis players. There's no doubt they possessed sporting skills – his father was an accomplished skier and football player while his mother studied sport at university – but Novak admits: "It's no accident that I ended up playing sport, but it is a little bit odd that I started playing tennis." No one else he knew played tennis. No one he knew had even attended a professional tennis match. What's more, at that time, tennis was still a fairly minor sport in Serbia.

BELOW: Panoramic view over the Banjica neighborhood in Belgrade, where the Djokovic family lived.

> "When you are that young, you believe in everything. You live through your dreams and your dreams are your reality. You have that moment of, let's say, a revelation when you just know that one day it is going to be you holding that trophy."
>
> Novak Djokovic

In his autobiography, Novak realises how fortuitous it was to have this tennis academy so close to his home. "Some higher power was surely at work," he wrote.

Still a tiny kid, just six years old, he would stand for hours beside those academy courts, watching through the chain-link fence as other youngsters practised. He says he was "transfixed" by the rhythm of the balls flipping back and forth across the nets.

His curiosity didn't go unnoticed. One day the head coach at the academy approached him, inviting him to come back the following day and join in – this was his first meeting with Jelena Genčić.

What happened next was perhaps an indication of the highly organised and professional athlete he would one day grow to become. The next day, Novak arrived carrying an enormous tennis kit bag. Inside was all the clothing and equipment you'd expect an adult match player to bring along to a practice session. There was a racket, of course, but also a towel, a spare shirt, wristbands, a water bottle and balls, all neatly packed.

LEFT: Novak's father Sdrjan supported his son from the beginning, contributing to many successes, including this one at Wimbledon in 2019.

Genčić naturally assumed his mother had prepared the bag for him but, no, Novak insisted it was all his own initiative. It was mid-summer and he'd been watching the world's top players on TV as they competed at Wimbledon. Just like them, he wanted to have all the essential kit he'd need to be a champion. (Twenty years later, Novak admitted to Genčić that it was in fact his mother who had packed the bag that day, but that he had instructed her what to place in it after seeing Wimbledon players do the same.)

Genčić was immediately impressed by the precocious youngster. She alerted the other coaches to his potential. In particular she noticed his attentiveness, concentration and excellent motor skills.

That same day, Genčić walked across the road to meet Novak's parents at the pizzeria. "You have a golden child," she famously told them. She predicted that, by the time he was 17, he would be ranked among the top five best players in the world. (As it turned out, she was wrong by only a couple of years: Novak entered the world top five on April 30th 2007, at the age of 19.)

Watching Wimbledon as a youngster had a huge influence on Novak. It was around the time of his first meeting with Genčić that he was first exposed to the exploits of the American legend Pete Sampras. At the 1993 Wimbledon championships, Sampras and fellow American Jim Courier contested the men's singles final.

In his book *Pete Sampras: Greatness Revisited*, sports writer Steve Flink interviewed Novak about his memories of that match. "The first video image of professional tennis I had was Pete winning this final over Courier in 1993," he said. "I was so amazed with his skills and his composure and the whole setting of watching him play on the most sacred court of the sport. I just fell in love with everything.

"When you are that young, you believe in everything. You live through your dreams and your dreams are your reality. You have that moment of, let's say, a revelation when you just know that one day it is going to be you holding that trophy. I really felt that day watching Pete that it was kind of a higher power instilled in me. I received that information from above. It is just one of those things that you can't explain. You just feel it and know it deep inside." Novak has always said that, growing up, Sampras was his greatest hero, and a huge influence on him.

Meanwhile, under the tutelage of Genčić, Novak's tennis skills were advancing apace. He practised long and hard and claims he never needed to be encouraged by his parents or coaches. Right from the very start he was a model student. Genčić was particularly impressed with Novak's footwork. His

ABOVE: Novak entered the top 5 for the first time on April 30th 2007, after winning his first round match at the Estoril Open.

RIGHT: Watching Sampras defeat Courier at Wimbledon in 1993 encouraged Novak to start taking his tennis very seriously.

ABOVE: Novak received extra attention from his father to ensure his professional success.

LEFT: Novak and brother Djordje competing in doubles at the 2015 China Open.

experience as a young skier meant his ankles and knees were extra-flexible. Translated onto the tennis court, this flexibility allowed him to move quickly and efficiently. Even on hard courts, he was able to slide into wide shots – by no means a simple technique. Novak also possessed huge stamina, often staying behind to practise after the other kids had gone home. His natural inquisitiveness ensured he regularly pressed Genčić for extra information about technique and tactics.

Genčić taught him a lot more than just tennis, though. "She became a partner with my family in my intellectual upbringing," he wrote in *Serve to Win*. Regularly she would tutor him in classical music, literature, poetry, art, even social etiquette. She encouraged him to study foreign languages – he can now converse confidently in English, German and Italian. As a child Genčić had learned the piano to a decent level, and she felt it her duty to introduce him to classical composers such as Frédéric Chopin, Claude Debussy and Edvard Grieg. He has often referred to her as his "tennis mother". Coaching him from the age of five to twelve, she clearly had an enormous influence on his personal and intellectual development.

And all the time, his mind was on his future as a professional tennis player, and a world champion. "I would take different cups or bowls or pieces of plastic as my trophy, stand in front of the mirror, and say, 'Nole is the champion! Nole is number one!'" he wrote in *Serve to Win*.

Novak's father rarely gives interviews, which is a shame because when he does talk in public he's bold in stating his often controversial views. In 2016 he granted a rare audience to the American magazine *Newsweek*.

"He was the first child. He was welcomed with a lot of love, because he was the first grandson and son," he said. "The difference between us and Western countries – when we have a child, we want to be in its life 100 per cent until the end. That's why in Serbia and the Balkans we are so connected with our children. There is some special, unconditional love we have toward each other."

Srdjan admits he lavished Novak with extra attention, to the detriment of his other two sons, Marko and Djordje. "All throughout Novak's childhood, he was the most loved. Only Novak mattered. All of us – even his family and coaches – were unimportant. Everything was made for him to achieve what he has achieved today. Unfortunately for all the family, Marko and Djordje did not have one per cent of my enthusiasm, will and power that I gave to Novak. I am sad because of this, because Marko and Djordje could have achieved something great. The problem is Novak took all my energy; I had nothing left. I had no power left."

Both of Novak's younger brothers competed on the professional tour, but at a very low level in comparison to big brother. Given Srdjan's admissions of favouritism, it's possible that, had they been encouraged more by their father, they would have climbed the ATP rankings further. The reality is they were journeymen. The middle brother, Marko, enjoyed the more impressive career, competing on the tour – but mostly in lower-level Challenger and Futures tournaments – between 2007 and 2019, reaching career-high rankings of 571 in singles and 323 in doubles. In the latter, big bro teamed up with him a handful of times. Youngest brother Djordje also competed mainly in Challengers and Futures, but his career was shorter – from 2011 to 2015. His career-high rankings were 1,463 in singles and 559 in doubles.

Was Srdjan wise or unwise to focus all his attention on his first-born? Both of Novak's brothers are unremitting in their support for their eldest sibling. It certainly doesn't seem there's any bitterness lurking in the background.

Srdjan claims that Novak's future career path had been mapped out right from the start. "Since he was six, when he first started training, every aspect of his career has been taken care of," he told Newsweek. "What he's working on today, tomorrow, in a month and in a year; what he's eating, drinking, today, tomorrow, when he's going to school, what he got in a maths test, what his wishes and unfulfilled dreams are. Every aspect and every small thing in his life has been controlled. Why? Many talented children don't succeed, all around the world, because the parents are very unrealistic when it comes to their careers, lives and dreams. They decide their child is a great talent, and then put so much pressure on the child that it cannot handle it. When it grows up and learns how to live, there is chaos in the family, divorce – all the family is destroyed."

To say that parents of sports champions make enormous sacrifices on behalf of their offspring is something of a cliché. But it's almost always true. Srdjan and Dijana were no exception.

In the early years their financial situation was often rather bleak. The restaurant business and the sports shop would have brought in a small amount of money, but Western sanctions and bombings had decimated the Serbian economy. And, as every tennis parent knows to their chagrin, once you commit to propelling your tennis-playing child towards the professional game, the bills mount up fast and furiously.

Novak's parents weren't naïve. They knew they needed a sizeable war chest for all the coaching and travel costs that would inevitably bite.

In his autobiography, Novak explains how, even before his junior tennis career

OPPOSITE: A young Djokovic in action during the 2005 Australian Open.

had started, in a time of war, his parents were already scrimping and borrowing just to put food on the table. "My father was borrowing money everywhere he could to keep us living the same life we had always known," he wrote. "We were surrounded by death, but he did not want us to know that, did not want us to know how poor we were." He remembers one evening when his father placed a German banknote on the kitchen table – just 10 Deutschmarks – and announced to the family that this was all the money they had left in the world.

BELOW: Dijana and Sdrjan Djokovic worked hard to provide for their family while Novak was building his career.

At the height of the NATO bombings, Belgrade households were lucky to receive more than a few hours of electricity a day. Novak recalls how his mother would be ready to cook the family meal the second the power came through, knowing it wouldn't last long. "We had at least soup and sandwiches to eat," he wrote.

Money became even tighter as Novak's tennis expenses grew. In a 2010 interview with a Serbian TV station, Srdjan explained just how difficult life became. He claims he and his wife were working 15-hour days, and that they sold off the family jewellery. Sometimes there was no money for food. Apparently they were forced to borrow cash from ruthless loan sharks at monthly interest rates of up to 15 per cent. More than once, unable to pay the interest on time, Srdjan was threatened with a knife held to his throat.

Despite these hardships, Novak's junior career soon thrived. But as is the case with many future adult champions, it wasn't exactly what you'd call a stellar junior record. He won two ITF junior tournament titles, both in 2002. His greatest moment was probably reaching the semi-finals of the Australian Open juniors in 2004, after which he gained a junior world ranking of 24. By this time, he was already flirting with lower-level tournaments on the adult tour.

Like so many tennis dads, Srdjan was scrabbling around for sponsorship for his talented son. Many times he has complained that the Serbian tennis federation offered no financial help, despite Novak's obvious potential. "There was no goodwill for anyone to help us, even though Novak was becoming a great player. I had to do it all by myself," he said in the *Newsweek* interview. "For ten years, I was never apart from him. We were always together. Everywhere we went, everybody else had a team – physios and coaches. Everybody else was taken care of, except us. I was Novak's mother, father, coach, physio ... everything."

Salvation came in the form of two Israeli sports agents, Amit Naor and Allon Khakshouri. The former was a professional player in the 1980s, while the latter has since ended up staging several ATP tennis events. In 2003, when Novak was 16 years old, they signed a deal with Srdjan – reported by some media outlets to be worth as much as 250,000 euros a year. Whatever the amount, it meant the Djokovic family's money worries were over.

By now, Novak had dipped his toes into professional tennis. His first ever match as an adult was at a Futures tournament in Munich, in January 2003, where he lost to a German player ranked in the 600s, called Alex Rădulescu. Ignominious start it may have been, but glory wasn't long coming. By June that year he had won his first Futures tournament – in Serbia, as it happens. Two years

later he found himself competing for the first time in the main draw of a Grand Slam, at the 2005 Australian Open. By July 2005 he'd cracked the world top 100. In 2006, in the Netherlands, he'd won his first title on the ATP tour.

Novak would never be poor again.

ABOVE: Novak celebrating his first title on the ATP tour, after defeating Nicolás Massú at the final of the 2006 Dutch Open.

ALL-TIME NUMBER OF MATCHES WON

In terms of all-time wins on the ATP tour, Djokovic is very close to the summit.*

* After 2023 US Open

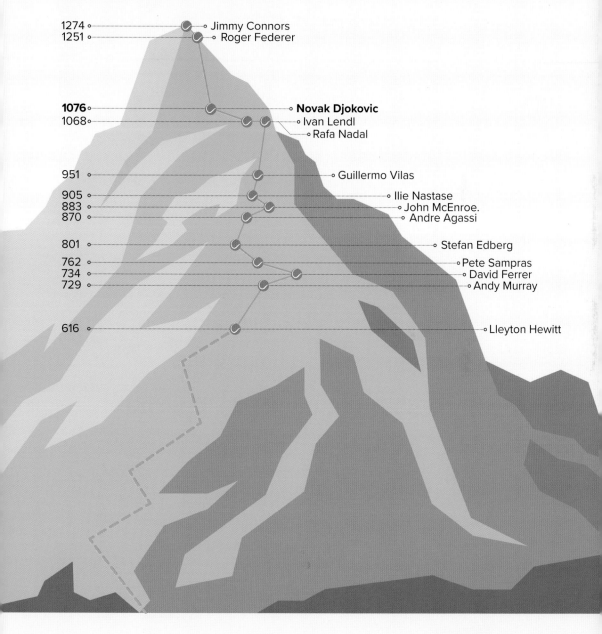

1274 ○ ⋯⋯⋯⋯⋯⋯⋯⋯⋯⋯⋯ ○ Jimmy Connors
1251 ○ ⋯⋯⋯⋯⋯⋯⋯⋯⋯⋯⋯ ○ Roger Federer

1076 ○ ⋯⋯⋯⋯⋯⋯⋯⋯ ○ **Novak Djokovic**
1068 ○ ⋯⋯⋯⋯⋯⋯⋯⋯ ○ Ivan Lendl
  ○ Rafa Nadal

951 ○ ⋯⋯⋯⋯⋯⋯⋯⋯⋯ ○ Guillermo Vilas

905 ○ ⋯⋯⋯⋯⋯⋯⋯⋯⋯ ○ Ilie Nastase
883 ○ ⋯⋯⋯⋯⋯⋯⋯⋯⋯ ○ John McEnroe.
870 ○ ⋯⋯⋯⋯⋯⋯⋯⋯⋯ ○ Andre Agassi

801 ○ ⋯⋯⋯⋯⋯⋯⋯⋯⋯ ○ Stefan Edberg

762 ○ ⋯⋯⋯⋯⋯⋯⋯⋯⋯ ○ Pete Sampras
734 ○ ⋯⋯⋯⋯⋯⋯⋯⋯⋯ ○ David Ferrer
729 ○ ⋯⋯⋯⋯⋯⋯⋯⋯⋯ ○ Andy Murray

616 ○ ⋯⋯⋯⋯⋯⋯⋯⋯⋯ ○ Lleyton Hewitt

THE MATCH

DUTCH OPEN

July 23rd 2006

Amersfoortse Lawn Tennisclub, Amersfoort, Netherlands

Final: Novak Djokovic beat Nicolás Massú 7–6, 6–4

Back in 2006, Novak was already turning heads, one of the more impressive teenagers plying his trade on the ATP tour. By the summer of that season, he had already reached the quarter-finals at Roland Garros and the fourth round at Wimbledon, and was ranked at 36 in the world. All of which secured him the number three seed at the Dutch Open, in the city of Amersfoort.

Hungry to make his mark, the 19-year-old wasn't about to waste any opportunities. In fact, he didn't lose a single set all week. In the semi-final he wasn't even required to complete the match, as his Argentinian opponent, the top seed Guillermo Coria, was forced to retire after just nine games with a neck injury.

By the time Novak reached the final against Chilean player Nicolás Massú – ranked 37 in the world – he was displaying impressive, forceful tennis. Back in those days he was clothed in Adidas kit and using Wilson rackets. Looking confident, he broke serve first, soon pushing ahead to a 4–1 lead. Massú remained calm, though, and with some strong serving managed to level the score. That first set culminated in a tiebreak which Novak edged through, winning 7–5.

In the second set, Massú initially took control. But Novak was soon back on top. After winning four games in a row, he sealed the second set and victory after two hours and 19 minutes – his first ever title on the ATP tour. Cheering courtside were his coach Marián Vajda and his girlfriend (now his wife) Jelena Ristić. The victory saw him rise eight places in the world rankings, into the top 30 for the first time.

Several years later, Massú remembered Novak's maiden title fondly. The Chilean claimed that the teenager had impressed him enormously.

"Djokovic stood out at his age," he said. "His strength, similar to Roger Federer's, was growing up really fast. He faced me as an equal. We had already trained beforehand, but in the match his spectacular potential was noticeable."

I thought he'll surely be in the top five in the future. He had it all: the game and a winning mentality. During many critical moments, he kept focused and he didn't let me win."

Interestingly, when the Dutch Open came to an end, after the 2008 edition, there was a spare week in the ATP calendar. A Serbian company called Family Sport purchased the slot and launched Serbia's first ever ATP event, a clay-court tournament in Belgrade called the Serbia Open. And guess who ran Family Sport back then? The Djokovic family, of course. Novak's uncle, Goran, was the original tournament director.

BELOW: Aged 19, Novak was desperate to secure his first ATP tournament title.

He [Djokovic] faced me as an equal. We had already trained beforehand, but in the match his spectacular potential was noticeable. I thought he'll surely be in the Top 5 in the future.

Nicolás Massú

LEFT: Novak serves to Massú in the Dutch Open final.

2
NOVAK
THE SERB

What does Serbia mean to Novak, and what does Novak mean to Serbia? The two entities – one a globally famous sporting superstar, the other a small land-locked nation in southeast Europe – are closely intertwined, sometimes in rather complicated ways.

The politics of the Balkans are never straightforward, and Novak should be commended for navigating them mostly very diplomatically. (Not so his father Srdjan – more of that later.) There never existed such problems for Switzerland's Roger Federer or Spain's Rafa Nadal.

The aim of this book is not to examine Serbian politics in depth. However, a glimpse into the background of Novak's home nation is essential if we wish to understand both the man and the player.

Novak is Serbian through and through. He was born in the capital, Belgrade, to two parents also born in Serbia. According to Chris Bowers, author of *Novak Djokovic: The Biography*, Novak's paternal grandparents, also ethnic Serbs, hail from Montenegro, while his maternal grandparents, both officers in the Yugoslav army before the break-up of Yugoslavia, were originally from the eastern part of Croatia, near the border with Serbia. His family name is actually spelt Đoković. In its westernised form, the accents are dropped and a j is added after the D to create the spelling Djokovic that we now all know so well.

Within the various separate nations of the former Yugoslavia, ethnic and national heritage are both complicated and a matter of vehement pride, especially after the Yugoslav Wars of the 1990s. Novak is no exception. He has always professed a great love and patriotism for his native Serbia.

It's not an unreasonable generalisation to say that citizens who feel a threat to their national identity are often more patriotic – even nationalistic – than citizens of more established nations. So it's worth bearing in mind that, while

the Serbs trace their ethnic heritage back to the Slavic migrations of the sixth century BC, they have existed as an independent sovereign state only three times: once during the Middle Ages; from 1878 to the end of the First World War in 1918; and from 2006 to the present day.

No wonder then that Novak is lionised, almost worshipped, by his countrymen as a leading statesman and symbol of national pride. In understanding Novak and his place in the world, this fact cannot be underestimated: right now he is far and away the most famous person in Serbia, more famous even than the nation's president or prime minister. The patron saint of Serbia might be Sava, but Novak would give him a good run for his money.

Saša Ozmo is a tennis journalist with Balkan TV channel and website Sport Klub, and has observed Novak's progress on the tennis court keenly over the years. "I'd say he is pretty patriotic. He is not nationalist by any measure but, yes, he is patriotic. In the earlier part of his career he was even more open with [nationalism] on the international stage. Now he always says one of the favourite moments of his career was after he won Wimbledon in 2011 and 100,000 people gathered in one of the main squares in Belgrade." Ozmo also points to Serbia's triumph in the Davis Cup final in 2010, and the way Novak evidently relished his role in it.

The line between patriotism and nationalism is a fine one and, over the years, Novak has learned to tread it very carefully indeed. At home in Belgrade, he does well to engage the support of his compatriots by competing in the Serbia Open (which his family company Family Sport owned and organised for several years), and by offering moral support to the Serbian diaspora scattered elsewhere among the Balkans. But when he's competing and travelling on the world stage, he realises he needs to be cautious not to ally himself too closely to Serbian nationalism. Serbia's reputation internationally is by no means spotless. Ever since the reign of the infamous Slobodan Milošević, who died in jail while being tried for war crimes and crimes against humanity during the Yugoslav Wars, Serbia has incurred the disapproval of many in Western Europe and the wider Western world.

In the 2021 podcast interview "In Depth with Graham Bensinger", Novak discussed his place in Serbia in detail. "I feel that through sport people get closer to each other," he said. "Sport has power to unite, as Nelson Mandela used to say, and I truly believe in that."

He pointed out how his success, along with the success of his Serbian sporting colleagues, has elevated the image of Serbia across the rest of the world, especially in the West. "I am happy to be part of that team and part of the contribution. You can say my success had a positive impact on the reputation of Serbia, for sure."

Asked what his nation means to him, he said the following: "Serbia is my cradle. Serbia is the country that allowed me to grow up into the person and tennis player I am today and for that I am eternally grateful to Serbia."

OPPOSITE: After winning the 2010 Davis Cup final, Novak and his Serbian teammates all had their hair cut off.

ABOVE: Young or old, Novak's appeal in Serbia is universal.

RIGHT: Novak celebrates with Serbian fans at the 2021 French Open.

LEFT: Novak's fans cheer as he becomes world number one in 2011.

> Serbia is my cradle. Serbia is the country that allowed me to grow up into the person and tennis player I am today and for that I am eternally grateful to Serbia.

Novak Djokovic

Cautiously diplomatic in his answers, he added the following: "I don't see my country or Serbia through the lens of politics. I see Serbia as a country, a mother to all of us that gave us life and gave us opportunity to grow into the people we are today. Serbia will forever be my home number one."

Interestingly, back in 2006, when Novak was just starting to win his first tournaments on the ATP tour and family finances were stretched to their limit, the governing body of tennis in Great Britain – the Lawn Tennis Association (LTA) – tried to encourage the youngster to switch to playing for Britain, with the promise of increased funding and better training facilities. Ultimately, they wanted to smooth the way for him to become a British citizen and move with his family to the UK. He turned them down, however.

Novak later explained how the LTA tried to woo him because, despite all the cash they had invested in tennis, through money earned from the All England Championships at Wimbledon, at the time they still only had one decent player – Andy Murray – to show for it. "That had to be a disappointment for all the money they invest," Novak explained. "But I didn't need the money as much as I had done. I had begun to make some for myself, enough to

afford to travel with a coach, and I said, 'Why the heck?' I am Serbian, I am proud of being a Serbian, I didn't want to spoil that just because another country had better conditions. If I had played for Great Britain, of course I would have played exactly as I do for my country, but deep inside, I would never have felt that I belonged."

In his interview with Graham Bensinger, he explained the LTA offer in further detail. "It was very tempting at that time for my parents because [they] would get a job; my family would get a house. It was a great, great deal."

But he added: "I personally didn't feel it from the beginning." He told his parents: "I don't want to go and live in England, I don't know anybody. I want to stay here with my friends. I have my school, I have my life, I have my country, I have my language, I have everything here." Just imagine how his life might have changed if he had accepted the offer.

Proud Serb and international sports star: Novak plays both roles with aplomb. At home, he knows how to curry favour with his compatriots, and when abroad, he often brilliantly plays the diplomat and statesman. The one notable exception to this was the Covid vaccine debacle (see Chapter 8), which for a while risked damaging his international image beyond repair.

The other spanner in the works is Novak's father Srdjan. Although giving few on-the-record interviews, he has a reputation for voicing rather eccentric opinions. In the 2016 interview with American magazine *Newsweek*, for example, he suggested his son was so celebrated in his home nation as to be more important than Serbia itself. "He is the symbol of Serbia and a god of new Serbia, but this makes me sad," he said. "Novak is the only bright point at the end of the tunnel for Serbia at the moment. I am very worried about the country and the people; what is going to happen after Novak ends his career. The people of Serbia see Novak as their idol for how to succeed. He is the living example of how to achieve the impossible with your family around you. But there is nothing for Serbia except him."

In 2023, during the Australian Open, Srdjan inadvertently embarrassed his son by appearing outside the tournament's main arena with a group of pro-Vladimir Putin supporters who were waving Russian flags and chanting messages of support for the Russian leader. Novak was quick to defend his father, claiming the

supporters had "mis-used" his father. "I'm sorry that that has escalated so much. But I hope people understand that there was absolutely no intention whatsoever to support any kind of war initiatives or anything like that."

Srdjan himself later said: "I am here to support my son only. I had no intention of causing such headlines or disruption. I had no intention of being caught up in this. My family has lived through the horror of war, and we wish only for peace."

It's all further proof, however, of just how cautious Novak and his family need to be when politics are involved.

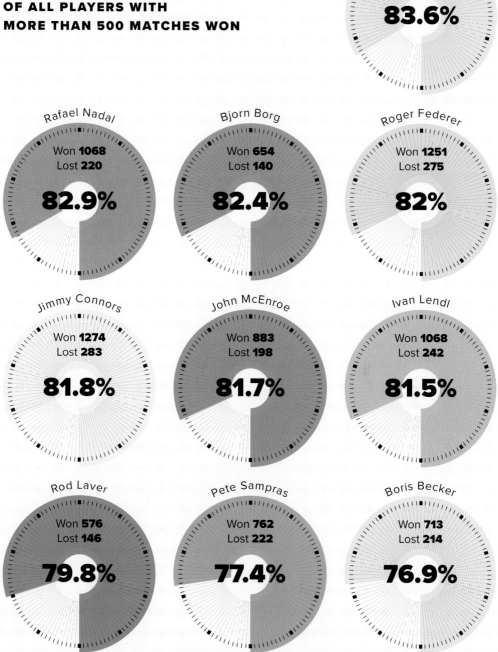

**BEST WINNING PERCENTAGE
OF ALL PLAYERS WITH
MORE THAN 500 MATCHES WON**

Novak Djokovic
Won **1076**
Lost **211**
83.6%

Rafael Nadal
Won **1068**
Lost **220**
82.9%

Bjorn Borg
Won **654**
Lost **140**
82.4%

Roger Federer
Won **1251**
Lost **275**
82%

Jimmy Connors
Won **1274**
Lost **283**
81.8%

John McEnroe
Won **883**
Lost **198**
81.7%

Ivan Lendl
Won **1068**
Lost **242**
81.5%

Rod Laver
Won **576**
Lost **146**
79.8%

Pete Sampras
Won **762**
Lost **222**
77.4%

Boris Becker
Won **713**
Lost **214**
76.9%

THE MATCH

AUSTRALIAN OPEN

January 27th 2008

Melbourne Park, Melbourne, Australia

Final: Novak Djokovic beat Jo-Wilfried Tsonga 4–6, 6–4, 6–3, 7–6

B y 2008, the world was desperate for a new male champion. For the previous four years, the Grand Slams had been utterly dominated by the twin axis of Roger Federer and Rafa Nadal, with only two major titles resisting their stranglehold. So when Novak started flexing his muscles, fans began to get excited.

The previous season he had reached the semi-finals at Roland Garros and Wimbledon, the final at the US Open, and had won a couple of ATP Masters events. Going into the 2008 Australian Open, his ranking was bubbling at a very impressive number three in the world. But could he thwart the domination of the Spaniard and the Swiss ranked above him?

Right from the start, his Melbourne campaign showed he was confident, aggressive and fleet of foot. En route to the final, he lost not a single set, occasionally pushing opponents aside with apparent ease. Victims included local hero Lleyton Hewitt in the fourth round, world number five David Ferrer in the quarter-finals, and a stunned Roger Federer, world number one, in the semis. By the time he'd reached the final, to tackle the big-hitting Frenchman Jo-Wilfried Tsonga, his game was alight.

In that first set in the Rod Laver Arena, Novak was finally tested. Tsonga, whose heavy groundstrokes had been battering opponents all fortnight, quickly asserted his authority. Winners came from all parts of the court and Novak's frustration was apparent. He seemed annoyed at his inability to keep the ball in play; annoyed at his own mistakes; annoyed at his erratic first serve; annoyed at the umpire, who he believed was refusing to overrule the line judges; annoyed at his father Srdjan, who at one point walked out of the arena; and annoyed at the very partisan crowd who were backing the Frenchman. At times, the more numerous Tsonga fans and the much smaller contingency of Novak fans attempted to drown each other out. You'd have been forgiven for thinking this might have been a Davis Cup tie between France and Serbia.

OPPOSITE: Novak and Tsonga in action during the final in the Rod Laver Arena.

> "With the way I was playing throughout all the junior years and junior events, I think I earned enough confidence and motivation to be a professional tennis player and to be a Grand Slam champion."
>
> Novak Djokovic

Before long it was France's man who had taken the first set 6–4, with a beautiful lob from his baseline.

From then on, Novak rediscovered the momentum that had propelled him to this Grand Slam final. The second set went his way, as did the third. At the start of the fourth set, he won the game to love. Then at 2–2, there was disquiet in the Serb's camp as he was forced to call the trainer for treatment on cramp incurred after chasing down a sneaky dropshot from Tsonga.

That fourth set raged on, eventually requiring a tiebreak. Aggressive as ever, Tsonga continued to play risky tennis. Two attempted winners were thwarted by the net, and then he served a double fault. Novak played more coolly, racing to 6–2 in the tiebreak, until finally Tsonga sent an inside-out forehand wide. Victory was Novak's. He dropped backwards, lay down on the court, placed his head in his hands and relished his very first Grand Slam title.

In the press conference afterwards, he attributed his win to a combination of self-belief and familial support. "I always believed, you know, I always believed. I didn't want to think in a negative way. I always had a big support, especially from

ABOVE: Novak didn't drop a single set on his way to the final.

ABOVE: Fans sided more with Frenchman Tsonga.

my parents, my father – you know, I think he always believed more in me than I did in myself.

"With the way I was playing throughout all the junior years and junior events, I think I earned enough confidence and motivation to be a professional tennis player and to be a Grand Slam champion. And it was difficult to judge in that time because Serbia doesn't have such a big tennis tradition. Considering all these bad times ... when I grew up. So it was basically impossible, if you look in that way. But I always believed."

Novak conceded that for a nation as small as Serbia, with few tennis facilities, his victory was all the more unusual. "I think everybody was really surprised with the amount of the players we produced from such a small country with no tennis tradition. Because there was no system whatsoever in our country for tennis, and we didn't get so much support. I think this hunger for success and the times and things we went through made us stronger."

THE TEAM
BEHIND
THE CHAMP

In March 2022, when he and his coach Marián Vajda mutually decided to part company, Novak posted this message on social media: "What a journey, Marián. 15 years! You have been by my side during the most important and memorable moments. We have achieved the unachievable and I will forever be grateful for your friendship and dedication. You will always be my family and I can't thank you enough for everything." The duo had started working together in June 2006 and, aside from a brief hiatus, were together for 15 years. The Slovakian, a former top 40 singles player in the 1980s, guided his charge to a score of Grand Slam triumphs, and 85 titles in all. If you measure a tennis coach's success by the number of Grand Slam singles titles he assists, then Vajda is possibly the most successful of all time. He and Novak are one of the greatest ever partnerships in professional tennis.

By the time of their split, Novak was already employing former Wimbledon champion Goran Ivanišević as an adviser, so that the transition to the next stage of his career was seamless. Ivanišević, a Croatian who reached number two in the world in 1994, is still Novak's current coach. "It is great to work with such a great athlete and player, but very demanding also," he once explained. "A final is not good enough. You need to win. We only count victories. We only count Slams. That is huge stress. But I choose that. I love it. It pushes me to learn more and be a better coach and a better person. I really enjoy it."

Very few tennis players get to both compete and coach at the very highest level, like Ivanišević. The Croat believes it's easier to make a living on the court than from the sidelines. "It's much easier to play because you play for yourself," he once told the ATP. "You get your frustrations and emotions out on the court. As a coach, you're sitting there, especially coaching a player for whom a final is not good enough. Only victories count. When you get into the machine, there

simply isn't room for error. You have to be switched on all the time. There is always something happening; we are nervous 24 hours a day. Nothing is ever alright. But then good things happen. Then it's all worth it."

The rest of Novak's support team are familiar faces. His physios are Miljan Amanovic (born in Croatia and one of his best friends) and Claudio Zimaglia, an Italian former long-jumper. His fitness trainer is Marco Panichi, another Italian, who has been working with him since 2017. In fact, Italians feature strongly in Novak's team. His two managers, Edoardo Artaldi (known as "Dodo") and Elena Cappellaro, both hail from Italy.

The impact of these latter two, whose function is to ease Novak's passage through professional life, should not be underestimated. He first met Artaldi back in 2008 when he joined in a sponsorship deal with the Italian clothing brand Sergio Tacchini. "We basically live together," Artaldi once told SBS Italian. "Elena and I try to create the atmosphere he needs, given how much time he spends around the world and away from his family. We try to be as professional as possible, but now our relationship is rather personal. We live together 24/7."

ABOVE: Novak with his Italian fitness trainer Marco Panichi.

OPPOSITE LEFT: Physiotherapist Miljan Amanovic is also one of Novak's best friends.

OPPOSITE RIGHT: Novak laughs with coach Ivanišević (far left) and manager Edoardo Artaldi.

The physio, Amanovic – nicknamed "Rodja" by Novak – first started working with the player in 2007. Arguably, he knows Novak's body better than anyone on the planet. For years he has rubbed, kneaded, prodded and manipulated the player's every muscle, joint and tendon. He attended Novak in the mornings, before matches, after matches, and plenty of times in between.

"Nole and I always have very open conversations because that's the only way we can function," he once explained. "He confides in me, I in him, and everything from that side is benevolent and sincere. Nole always likes to hear everything. Not only what I want to tell him, but he is willing to hear a lot of opinions before making a final decision for any situation."

In 2017, when Novak made wholesale changes to his support team, Amanovic stopped working with him. That same year, the physio suffered a heart attack, brought on, he said, by the stress of travelling full-time on the ATP tour.

"I survived a severe heart attack," he said after a full recovery. "I was resuscitated four times. Now I can say that it was God's will in the true sense of the word, because if only one link in the chain of events had not been in place that day, I would probably have left this earthly life. They say that they fought for me for 40 minutes."

Amanovic later rejoined Novak's support team for a second time. Nowadays, conscious to keep his stress levels as low as possible, he assists the player only part-time.

RIGHT: As well as Novak, Jelena Genčić coached many successful tennis players, including Ivanišević and Seles.

OPPOSITE: Novak teamed up with his hitting partner Gómez-Herrera at the 2021 Mallorca championships.

The final piece in the jigsaw is Novak's regular hitting partner who, currently, is Carlos Gómez-Herrera. No longer a full-time player, the Spaniard reached a career-high singles ranking of 268 in the world in 2018. In 2021 he teamed up with Novak for the doubles at a grass-court tournament in Mallorca, where they reached the finals but were forced to pull out after Gómez-Herrera injured his foot.

To really understand Novak, however, we need to go right back to the start of his coaching. Arguably, the tennis coach who wielded the most influence on Novak was his childhood instructor Jelena Genčić. Taking the reins when he was just six years old, she shaped his playing style

during his formative years, laying the foundations long before he matured and developed into a professional player. She also educated him in all sorts of other areas, both social and academic (see Chapter 1, page 25).

Born in 1936, Jelena hailed from a successful Yugoslavian family, her father a lawyer, her aunt an artist, her great-uncle the country's interior minister. Jelena was passionate about sport, especially handball and tennis. In the former she competed as goalkeeper for the Yugoslavian national team, winning a bronze medal at the 1957 world championships; in the latter she won multiple national titles and even dabbled in the Grand Slams. The apogee of her tennis-playing career was in 1959 when she played a handful of matches at Wimbledon in singles, doubles and mixed doubles.

Even before she finished playing competitive tennis, Jelena had already started coaching at a low level. Then she was invited to take a senior administrative role in tennis at her sports club, Partizan Belgrade. It was also around this time that she embarked on a career in TV production, focusing mainly on cultural programmes.

By the 1980s, Jelena was an important force in the development of junior players within Yugoslavia. For a while she guided two youngsters who would later become Grand Slam champions – Monica Seles and Goran Ivanišević, the latter

Novak's current coach, of course. Seles has praised Jelena's work in tennis, especially her role in promoting female athletes in a domain and society that was very male-dominated at the time.

It was in the early 1990s, when Novak was a complete beginner, that Genčić then turned her attention to him. She later said she knew, very early on in her tutorship, that she had a future world champion on her hands, recalling how her young protégé would often talk about winning Wimbledon and becoming world number one. "I remember showing him some trophies at my house," Genčić once said. "He said to me: 'Do you think I will win trophies like this one day?' I told him: 'Of course – and you will need a big house to put them all in.'" For years, the two were inseparable, spending hours both on and off the court together. Novak called her his "tennis mother".

Years later, when Novak was contesting the 2013 French Open in Paris, he received the sudden news that Genčić had died of a heart attack. She had been on court coaching juniors just days before. The shock to Novak was obvious to see. As he came off court after winning his fourth-round match, he used a marker pen to write a message on the TV camera. "Jeco love you forever," it said, making reference to his nickname for Genčić.

ABOVE: As a youngster, Novak attended a tennis academy in Munich run by former Croatian player Niki Pilić.

RIGHT: Australian Dejan Petrović was Novak's first coach as a professional player.

OPPOSITE: Ivanišević has both played and coached at the highest level.

"It hasn't been easy, but this is life," he said shortly afterwards. "Life gives you things, takes away close people in your life, and Jelena was my first coach, like my second mother. We were very close throughout my whole life, and she taught me a lot of things that are part of me, part of my character today, and I have [the] nicest memories of her. This is something that will stay forever and hopefully I will be able to continue on and follow up where she stopped, with her legacy, because she left so much knowledge to me and to the people that were close to her. She never got married, she never had kids, so tennis was all she had in life. She's one of the most incredible people I ever knew. She was an incredibly intelligent woman. She knew exactly to recognise the potential of the tennis players. That's why she, for me, is the best coach for that young generation that I ever met in my life."

Genčić's funeral took place two days after her death, on the second Monday of Roland Garros, and Novak was upset he couldn't attend. He sent a letter, however, which his mother read out at the service. It included the following words:

"Thank you for your patience, your enormous love. Thank you for your everyday support, for the advice I remember, for the warm words which always carried an extraordinary message. You know that I've memorised them all and that I always follow your rules. You were an angel. Both when you coached me and afterwards, I felt your support wherever I went. Sincere, strong, unconditional. You left an indelible mark on Serbian tennis. Everyone who holds a racket in his or her hands today is indebted to you. I promise I will speak your name to future generations and that your spirit will live on on our tennis courts."

By 1999, Novak's parents had realised their son needed to look outside of Serbia in order to take his game to the next level. Partly on Genčić's recommendation, they decided to send him to a tennis academy in Munich, operated by the Croatian former professional player Niki Pilić. Famous for sparking a players' boycott of the Wimbledon championships in 1973, Pilić coached teenagers looking to transition to the professional game. Novak was only 12 at the time and, initially, the coach was reluctant to take him on. But Genčić talked him into it. And straight away Pilić was impressed by the youngster's commitment.

At first Novak attended the academy part-time, staying with the Pilić family in Munich but regularly returning to Belgrade. Novak had other coaches back at the Partizan club – Bogdan Obradović, for example, and Ladislav Kis. Later, Novak moved to Munich to attend Pilić's academy full-time.

It wasn't until 2004, though, that Novak employed his first coach as a professional player. This was Dejan Petrović, an Australian national whose parents were Serbian. Petrović had plans to return to the mother country and open a tennis academy. The promising 17-year-old he found himself looking after was just the boost he needed to make his name in Serbia. And, indeed, it was under Petrović's tutelage that Novak advanced from the lowest level of the ATP tour – Futures tournaments – to the tour proper. The two only worked together for ten months but by the time they parted company, Novak had risen from a world ranking of 270 into the top 100. He was on the way to making his mark in pro tennis.

From then on, Novak galloped through a miscellany of coaches, some advising for several seasons, others dropped within months. While Marián Vajda provided him stability – guiding him between 2006 and 2022, with a short break in 2017 – there were multiple others. Some travelled with him full-time while others were brought on board in order to arm Novak with specific skills. There was the Italian Riccardo Piatti, the Croats Ivan Ljubičić and Mario Ančić, the Australian doubles legend Mark Woodforde, the American former world number four Todd Martin, the Serbian Dušan Vemić and the Czech Radek Štěpánek. In the 2010s Novak also employed two supercoaches, as they are known. Between 2013 and 2016, the German six-times Grand Slam winner Boris Becker was a regular in the player's box; and between 2017 and 2018 it was the American eight-times Grand Slam winner Andre Agassi.

Among all these coaches, aside from Vajda, it was arguably Becker who wielded the most influence over Novak. During the German's time at the helm – and before he went to jail in the UK, in 2022, for financial misconduct – Novak won six Grand Slams.

In an interview with Brian Rose, on the podcast and YouTube channel "London Real", Becker explained the closeness of his and Novak's relationship. "It became a very successful partnership. Ultimately it's always down to the player if he allows it. Some of these young superstars, they have everything – a lot of money in the bank – so they don't want to listen to the truth because life's good enough. So, I really compliment him for allowing me to say what I had to say, and for him to listen because he didn't need to. He was already an accomplished player. Yes, we ended up winning six majors together and it was great for him, great for me. But it started with him."

Becker explained how his relationship with Novak was "very sensitive, almost intimate". "Because I have to know everything about him," he added. "How he slept, how he ate, how he feels, how is his marriage ... everything matters because he carries that on a tennis court. That's his mindset, that's his psychology. Does he feel the pressure? Is he upset? Is he happy? Novak was able to share with me most of it and only because of that I was able to become a good coach. It took its toll on my life because you're married to the player. But that's the price you pay when you get involved in that scenario."

Before agreeing to coach Novak, Becker says he saw a grittiness in the Serb that reminded him of himself.

"I think we have similarities in character and personalities," he once explained. "I would call Novak a street fighter. When the going gets tough, when everything is against him, that's when he gets his best, and I'm similar. We're not the easiest of characters and we don't smile every day, but you can win the war with us."

Becker also pointed out how Novak is a perfectionist. "I think that's what drives him," he added. "He wants to get better every year. He wants to really create his own piece of history in the tennis world. He's not happy with number one or Grand Slam champion."

> A final is not good enough. You need to win. We only count victories. We only count Slams. That is huge stress. But I choose that. I love it. It pushes me to learn more and be a better coach and a better person.

Goran Ivanišević

DJOKOVIC-NADAL-FEDERER – HEAD TO HEAD RECORD AT GRAND SLAMS

Novak
Djokovic

Rafal
Nadal

Roger
Federer

	All Grand Slams	Australian	French	Wimbledon	US
Djokovic-Nadal	7-11	2-0	2-8	2-1	1-2
Djokovic-Federer	11-6	4-1	1-1	3-1	3-3
Federer-Nadal	4-10	1-3	0-6	6-3	0-0

THE MATCH

DAVIS CUP FINAL
December 5th 2010
Belgrade Arena, Belgrade, Serbia
Third singles rubber: Novak Djokovic beat Gaël Monfils 6–2, 6–2, 6–4

P olitics, terrorism, violence, cheating, even death threats ... there have been
some unforgettable Davis Cup ties over the decades. Fortunately, the
Davis Cup final in December 2010, between Serbia and France, will be
remembered not for nefarious reasons but for something much more mundane:
the haircuts.

Novak and his countrymen certainly displayed some very impressive tennis to
earn their victory, and the 17,000-strong home crowd at the Belgrade Arena were
ecstatic at the result, but it was when the entire team shaved all the hair off their
heads – fulfilling a promise they had made before the tie – that was the most
memorable episode.

That year's Serbia team, consisting of Novak, Janko Tipsarević, Viktor Troicki
and Nenad Zimonjić, had enjoyed a stellar run to the final, beating the United
States, Croatia and the Czech Republic. Their opponents in the final were France.

LEFT: The Serbian
Davis Cup team
(left to right):
Tipsarević, Zimonjić,
Troicki, Obradović
(coach), Novak and
Bozoljac (reserve).

OPPOSITE: Novak
celebrates his singles
victory over Monfils.

> After that Davis Cup win, I was full of life, full of energy, eager to come back to the tennis court, eager to play some more, win some other tournaments.

Novak Djokovic

LEFT: Novak stormed to victory in both his singles matches.

By the second day, France were leading 2–1, thanks to Gaël Monfils' singles victory over Tipsarević, and Michaël Llodra and Arnaud Clément's triumph in the doubles rubber. Serbia's only point was down to Novak's singles victory over Gilles Simon.

The next match was the reverse singles between Novak and Monfils, the most flamboyant player France had fielded in years. The Frenchman was renowned for his immense skill, but also for his tendency to show off during rallies with risky trick shots. Executed from all corners of the court, often at the most unexpected, even ill-advised moments, these shots might be played through his legs, behind his back, over his shoulder, with both feet off the ground, or at full stretch doing the splits.

Sure enough, in the fourth game of the first set, Monfils attempted to play a forehand in between his legs while leading 30–0. He missed it, damaged his racket by striking it on the hard court, and promptly lost the next four points to hand Novak the break of serve. Novak broke his opponent twice in each of the first two sets to lay down an impressive lead.

In the third set, Monfils began to look stronger, pushing back against his higher-ranked opponent and against the understandably deafening Belgrade supporters. It ended up being a catalogue of broken serves, with both players displaying their nerves until Novak eventually closed out the set for victory.

Throughout the entire match he allowed his opponent a grand total of just eight games. "It was unbelievable today," he said afterwards. "Under the circumstances, maybe one of the best matches I have played this year."

And the statistics proved his point. The Serbian played 18 unforced errors compared to Monfils' 37 – evidence of just what a risk-taker the Frenchman can be.

After tying the match at two rubbers all, it was left to Viktor Troicki to secure overall Davis Cup victory in the decisive singles match. To the delight of the thousands of cheering Belgradians, he pushed aside his French opponent Michaël Llodra 6–2, 6–2, 6–3 to give his nation the Davis Cup title for the first time in their history. The stadium filled with the raucous chants of "Serbia!" and "Viktor!"

Now it was time for the haircuts. As promised, all the team players, plus captain Bogdan Obradović, coach Niki Pilić and tennis federation president Slobodan Živojinović submitted themselves to the clippers; a hairdresser had been hired for the day and crewcuts were the only style he was offering. When it came to Novak's turn, first he was shaved in a stripe from forehead to the back of his head. Then a second stripe from ear to ear. Within seconds, the remainder of his hair was

ABOVE: The victorious Serbian team with their new haircuts.

lying on the tennis court around his feet. The employees of the International Tennis Federation looked a little nonplussed as they found themselves sweeping tufts of hair away with brooms from the trophy presentation stage.

Novak and the rest of his team first attended the official dinner before moving on to a club just off Republic Square in the centre of the capital where they all celebrated into the night, drinking champagne and smoking Cuban cigars, accompanied by a brass band playing traditional Serbian music. "This is the best moment of my career and probably of my nation," Novak said. "This is like winning the World Cup for us."

The players were now national heroes and were all awarded diplomatic passports the following spring.

The effect of the Davis Cup victory on Novak's individual game was quite phenomenal. The following year, his so-called *annus mirabilis*, saw him playing the finest tennis of his life. "After that Davis Cup win, I was full of life, full of energy, eager to come back to the tennis court, eager to play some more, win some other tournaments," he later reflected. "In a sentence, I lost my fear; I believed in my abilities more than ever."

THE PLAYING
STYLE OF A
CHAMPION

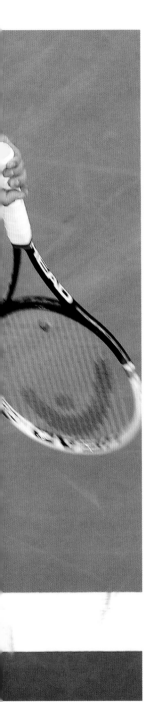

LEFT: Novak displays a professional attitude in every aspect of tennis.

What weapons does the world's greatest tennis player possess? What makes him so invincible on court? In the 20 years since he first embarked on the ATP tour, Novak's aggressive baseline game has developed spectacularly so that right now he possesses arguably the most effective backhand the sport has ever seen, especially when deployed with pace down the line. In addition, few players match him when it comes to the return of serve and court coverage.

Much of this is down to raw talent, but is also thanks to Novak's dedication to the job. Ever since that moment when, as a youngster, he presented himself to his first coach, Jelena Genčić, with a fully stocked kitbag, he has displayed a professional attitude to every aspect of his tennis.

Fellow Serbian player Viktor Troicki has watched his friend play since he was a kid. "Right at the start, he was very professional," he once explained in an interview in *Men's Health* magazine. "And I notice it now even more. He just does everything right. Everything. Watch him practise: he will give every session 100 per cent. It's not about practising for hours and hours, it's about practising right. He works on details: massage, strength, training, diet. He has a good, dedicated team and he can put all these things together to win the big titles."

NOVAK'S FITNESS

Close your eyes while watching a long rally between pros on a hard tennis court and one of the most noticeable sounds is the squeaking of the players' shoes as they chase around after the ball. When Novak is playing on a hard court, there's more squeaking than ever. His court coverage is faster, more athletic and more efficient than that of virtually every one of his peers. It's thanks to an unbelievably disciplined training regime.

Novak says he spends 14 hours a day either playing tennis, training for tennis, or eating. "That's what it takes to be

number one against the fittest and most competitive athletes in the world," he writes in his autobiography *Serve to Win*. "Constant, unyielding mental and physical preparation, 14 hours a day, seven days a week."

For Novak, everything hinges around his flexibility. All his fitness workouts start with 10 to 15 minutes of easy running (normally on a running machine) or easy cycling on a stationary bike in order to warm up his muscles. This is followed by a lengthy period of dynamic stretching – that's stretching while exercising. The exercises he uses include jumping jacks, walking with high knees, squat thrusts, lunges, and walking bent over with his palms on the floor. Years of doing this stretching has given Novak the kind of flexibility you'd find in a gymnast's body. And if you want proof, just look at his famous leg splits. It's almost painful to watch him as he executes the splits – both legs splayed wide and his undercarriage almost on the floor – in his attempts to reach a wide ball.

Just as important as pre-match stretching is post-match recovery. Novak will regularly finish a match close to midnight, sometimes with another match scheduled for the following day. In between tournaments he will put himself through gruelling training sessions both on and off the court. He will receive massages almost every day to help his muscles recover and his body to process the toxins that build up. "I think of massage as a necessity, not a luxury," he says.

OPPOSITE TOP: Each workout starts with 10–15 minutes of easy running.

OPPOSITE BOTTOM: Thanks to incredible flexibility, Novak can use leg splits to reach wider shots.

RIGHT: Novak receives treatment on court at Wimbledon.

And when he can't get a massage he uses a foam roller to administer self-massage. He swears by it. "You'll loosen tough connective tissue and decrease the stiffness of your muscles."

He is also a keen advocate of yoga, and at one point practised it every day. "Sometimes my back and hips stiffen up, and yoga is an amazing remedy for that," he says in his autobiography. "The breathing sequences also help me clear my mind. If my body tells me that I'm a little tight, or if I feel more stress than I'd like, I do a yoga session."

ABOVE: Supreme fitness allows Novak to stretch wide on both the forehand and backhand.

NOVAK'S BACKHAND

It's by far his most dangerous stroke. For his topspin backhand, Novak makes a brief split step before bringing his racket back with both hands – his right hand acting as the lead – and then stepping forward onto his right foot and bending his knees. He now strikes the ball low to high, in order to impart topspin, while shifting his body weight from his back foot to his front foot to propel extra energy into the ball. During contact with the ball, his head remains lowered, his eyes focused. His knees now straighten up, while his racket follows through all the way over his right shoulder and down his back so that the racket head almost ends up touching the small of his back, just above his backside. After completing the shot, his body is back in perfect equilibrium, ready to face the next ball in the rally.

The backhand is most effective when played down the line. He will also play a sliced backhand when needed, but this time using his right hand to play it while his left hand flies out to the side in order to create perfect balance.

Even as a defensive stroke, Novak's backhand is quite phenomenal. Just watch how, on both clay and hard courts, he slides low and wide to return a defensive backhand – his legs splayed like those of a giraffe at a waterhole. Other players can achieve this on a clay court, but very few manage to slide on hard courts as Novak does. By skidding into the shot, he can recover much more quickly for the subsequent shot than if, as most players do, he were to take short, quick steps. Often he will play the return cross-court, into the opposite service box, turning defence into offence, and frustrating the hell out of his opponents in the process.

NOVAK'S FOREHAND

Thanks to his balletic footwork, Novak has the time and space to strike his forehands in either an open stance (with legs spread), or in a closed stance (with his right leg stepping forward into the shot).

He likes to hold his racket up high, with his left hand supporting the throat of the racket, until very late in the shot. When he finally takes the racket back, the stringbed is facing the ground, and he's wielding the racket with a grip somewhere between semi-western and full-western. This allows him to unleash immense power as his right arm whips up and through the shot, rolling over the ball as he strikes it – fairly early – in order to impart loads of topspin. His body rotation gives his forehand shots more power, too.

Novak uses different follow-through styles: sometimes a traditional follow-through, round to his left shoulder where he catches the racket throat with his left

hand; other times a buggy whip, which gives him extra topspin; occasionally his follow-through ends up down by his left hip.

So skilled is he that, often, he can turn a defensive forehand into an offensive one. One of the most effective examples of this is when he hits a forehand cross-court while on the run. It's a wonder to behold.

NOVAK'S SERVE

Early in his career, Novak's serve was something of a liability; certainly nothing you'd describe as a weapon. But by 2011, his *annus mirabilis*, he had drastically changed the takeback of his racket, bending his elbow much more. It resulted in far more power and a better percentage of service-game wins. The stats bear this out: in 2005, he produced an annual total of just 88 aces, but by 2012 he was regularly firing down close to 500 aces a year.

His current service action is a thing of beauty. It starts with a very steady ball toss using a straight left arm. Then his racket arm bends elegantly at the elbow before whipping up and over the falling ball, pronating his wrist and imparting topspin for the first serve. His shoulders rotate so that when he strikes the ball, it's with huge power. At the same time his legs propel him up into the

air and well over the baseline so that lands him a good step into the court after firing the serve.

The point of contact with the ball varies, depending on whether he's hitting flat or slice serves (the usual tactic for the first serve), or kick serves (the usual tactic for second serves). In the old days, like many players, Novak employed a classic kick serve on his second serve. Nowadays, though, it is usually more of a slice-kick combination.

In recent years, his service placement has been fairly regular. According to the ATP, when he's serving into the deuce court, he sends 47 per cent of his serves down the T, 48 per cent wide, and 5 per cent into the middle section of the service court. Serving to the advantage side, it's 45 per cent down the T, 48 per cent wide, and 7 per cent into the middle section. Over the course of his career, the most effective service placement of all has been down the T into the deuce service court – with a winning percentage of 76.8 per cent.

The coaching advice he has received from Goran Ivanišević – one of the most effective servers ever – has no doubt helped. This Croatian player, who won Wimbledon in 2001 thanks to his laser-like serve, believes Novak's serve is a stronger weapon than many give him credit for.

OPPOSITE: On the forehand he whips the racket up and through the ball to impart huge topspin.

ABOVE: Novak's serve used to be a weakness but, in recent years, he has perfected the technique.

NOVAK'S RETURN OF SERVE

Is he the best returner-of-serve tennis has ever known? Quite possibly. The key aspect to Novak's return of serve is the extra time he gives himself to play the ball. He faces serves with a wide, well-balanced stance, his feet wide apart, ensuring a fairly low centre of gravity, and a readiness to move lightning-fast to the forehand or the backhand. Holding the racket, he has a forehand grip on the lower hand, and a backhand grip on the upper hand. This means he can switch quickly to either forehand or backhand and strike the return shot without needing to swivel the racket grip too much. Again, it saves him time.

Before his opponent serves, Novak is particularly shrewd in seeking telltale signs as to where the serve is likely to land. Years of experience have given him the ability to read serves with precision. He watches his opponent's ball toss, and the position of the legs and body. Once the ball leaves the server's racket, Novak tracks it like a hawk. Then, instinctively, he makes a split-step, jumping up on both feet. Immediately after landing, he pushes off to the forehand or backhand side, depending on which way the ball is coming. This gives him an extra split-second to prepare for the return. Then he lunges forward into his shot. By shortening his backswing, again, he gives himself extra time to cut off his opponent's serve. (On slower clay courts or against weaker serves he may have time to take a longer backswing.) The momentum of his body moving forward then imparts extra power into his return shot.

NOVAK'S MENTAL GAME

Novak says he uses several mental techniques to keep him "sharp, focused and dialled-in during both practice and matches". At tournaments, he claims to draw energy from his fans, especially the younger ones. "I go out of my way to meet fans, sign autographs, and pose for pictures," he writes in *Serve to Win*. "Yes, it's a nice thing to do for them, but it also serves me well. I draw tremendous positive energy from crowds like that, and I need that positive energy to succeed. People

OPPOSITE: His most effective service placement is down the T into the deuce service court.

ABOVE: He faces serves with a wide stance and a low centre of gravity.

RIGHT: Playing a sliced backhand in the 2021 Davis Cup semi-final.

DJOKOVIC'S SUCCESS TIMELINE

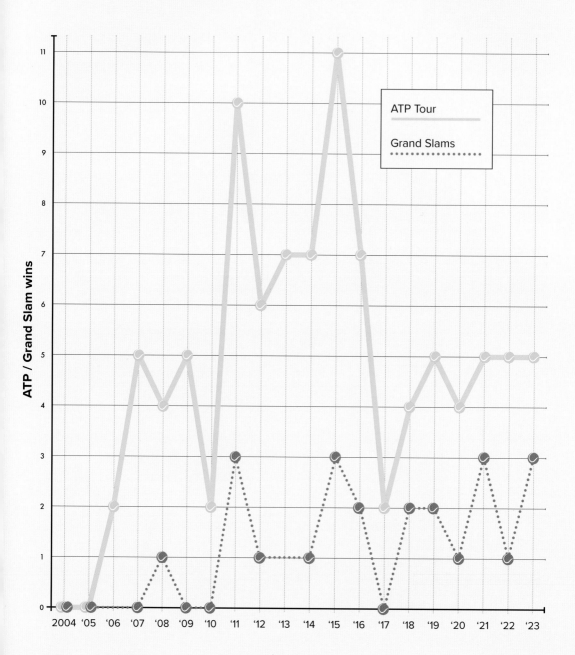

who cheer for me, who stop me to say hi, have no idea how important they are to my success."

Not everyone cheers for him, though. When he's up against Rafa Nadal, or when he used to play Roger Federer (now retired), Novak was always less popular with the fans – except when competing in his native Balkans, of course.

Imagine what it feels like to be up against Federer or Nadal, with the lion's share of the stadium chanting your opponent's name, applauding his every winning shot. It's almost as intimidating as competing away in a Davis Cup tie. In response, Novak devised an ingenious psychological tactic to get round the problem of being the unpopular player on the court. He trained himself to imagine that when the crowd started chanting his opponent's name, they were actually all chanting his own name. "It's a mechanism. It might sound weird, because obviously everyone is saying 'Roger!' or 'Rafa', or whatever it is. And I hear that, of course. But part of me inside says 'Okay, I'm not going to let that bring [me] down.'"

ABOVE: The buggy whip follow-through gives his forehand shots loads of topspin.

Novak uses some sort of reverse psychology to pretend he's the favourite player instead of the less popular player. "I try to transfer that into something that is useful to me," he explains. That way, he avoids feeling "bad, angry or upset" when the fans are all pitched against him.

Meditation has served Novak very well too. He admits that, in the past, during matches, he used to suffer from enormous self-doubt. Having practised meditation for many years, he now knows how to combat that self-doubt. He says he acknowledges the negative thoughts, letting them slide by, and focuses on the moment instead. "That mindfulness helps me process pain and emotions," he writes. "It lets me focus on what's really important. It helps me turn down the volume in my brain. Imagine how handy that is for me in the middle of a Grand Slam championship match." He says mindfulness has become one of his key philosophies in sport.

NOVAK'S RACKET

Among the higher-ranked professionals on the tour, not a single player uses a model of racket sold to the public. Nearly all of them customise them in certain ways. No serious elite player would dream of buying a new racket online or from a sporting goods shop and stepping straight out onto court with it. Like racing cars, all aspects of their weapons need to be fine-tuned to perfection. Some players have even been known to use a different brand of racket underneath their sponsor's paintjob. (There's no suggestion at all that Novak does this, however.)

The strings are the first area to receive attention. In virtually every country around the world (except the UK, for some strange reason) rackets are sold unstrung so that players can choose their own stringing set-up. Among the top pros, this is a highly complicated business, requiring experienced racket stringers who thread their player's rackets with strings in a specific material, gauge, pattern and tension.

Most players, Novak included, also use strips of lead to alter the weight, balance and head speed of their rackets, by sticking them to the frame. Some even open up the butt cap at the base of the racket handle and insert extra weight inside in the form of lead, silicone or epoxy.

OPPOSITE: When competing against the ever-popular Roger Federer, Novak used to pretend the fans were cheering for him instead.

ABOVE: Novak's racket sponsor won't reveal exactly which model he uses.

The handle itself is often different to the handle you'll see on rackets in the shops. Many pros are so meticulous in their demands that they ask their racket technicians to change the ratio of the bevels on the handle, for example, or even the length of the handle in some cases.

So what precisely is the racket that Novak goes into battle with? It depends who you believe. When asked exactly which model he uses, his sponsors Head said the following: "Unfortunately we do not give out any information about the pro players' personal rackets." All they will say is that he endorses their SPEED racket series.

Without confirmation from his sponsor, his support team or Novak himself, it's difficult to guess which racket he currently plays with. However, several experts have suggested he uses a professional stock racket called the Head PT113B, painted up to look like a Head SPEED model. This is a limited racket mould, not available for retail sale to the public.

His model looks to have a head size of 95 square inches, a length of 27.1 inches, a strung weight of 353g, a string pattern of 18x19, and a grip size of 4 inches. Although his string set-up will vary depending on the temperature, altitude and court surface of each tournament, he generally uses Babolat Touch VS natural gut on the main strings and Luxilon Alu Power Rough on the cross-strings.

> I go out of my way to meet fans, sign autographs, and pose for pictures. Yes, it's a nice thing to do for them, but it also serves me well. I draw tremendous positive energy from crowds like that, and I need that positive energy to succeed.
>
> Novak Djokovic

THE MATCH

WIMBLEDON

July 3rd 2011

All England Club, London, UK

Final: Novak Djokovic beat Rafael Nadal 6–4, 6–1, 1–6, 6–3

N ovak was understandably ecstatic when he captured his very first Wimbledon title in July 2011. He exclaimed: "It is the best day of my life. This is the tournament I always dreamed of winning. I think I am still sleeping, still dreaming. When you're playing the best player in the world ... I had to be on top of my game. I played probably my best match on grass courts ever." For the previous eight summers, this Grand Slam had been dominated by Federer and Nadal. Finally, Novak was able to break their stranglehold on the All England Club grass courts.

That season had seen Novak in exceptional form. In Melbourne, in January, he had demolished the field to take his second Australian Open title. Then, in quick succession, he had won tournaments in Dubai, Indian Wells, Miami, Belgrade, Madrid and Rome. In four of those finals, it was Nadal he had triumphed over. He seemed unstoppable, and he was quickly cementing his position as Nadal's greatest nemesis.

So when he arrived in London to contest the Wimbledon championships, just imagine his confidence. By the time he reached the final (against Nadal again), he had wiped aside four top-50 players. More importantly, he was just about to reach the world number one spot for the first time.

The match started off much as a heavyweight boxing match might, with both players thumping away at each other mercilessly. It wasn't until the 10th game that serve was broken, with Novak taking the advantage. Despite overwhelming support for his Spanish opponent, the Serb managed to dominate the second set, racing ahead to close it out six games to one.

Nadal had been in positions as grave as this many times in his career. Reacting strongly, he pressurised Novak, who double-faulted in the first deuce game of the match to give the Spaniard a 5–1 lead. Minutes later Nadal had his first set under his belt.

But it was to be a short reprieve. Finally, after close to two and a half hours of

RIGHT: Novak kisses his first Wimbledon trophy.

hard-fought tennis, Novak watched as Nadal pushed his final backhand long, down the line. The Serb dropped backwards, collapsing in relief on the grass.

Up in the players' box, his coach Marián Vajda and his trainers locked arms together, leaping up and down in unison. His parents and two younger brothers embraced. Novak meanwhile gently launched his used rackets into the hands of applauding spectators. He then bent down to kiss the Centre Court grass, even nibbling some of it.

"I didn't know what to do for my excitement and joy," he explained afterwards. "I felt like an animal. I wanted to see how it tastes. It tastes good."

This match was without doubt a turning point in Novak's career. He explained how this maiden Wimbledon triumph was an enormous boost of self-confidence since it proved to him that the dominance of Federer and Nadal could be punctured at the uppermost level of the sport.

"We all know the careers of Nadal and Federer," Novak said shortly after the final. "They have been the two most dominant players in the world, the last five years. They have won most of the majors we are playing. So sometimes it did feel frustrating when you get to the later stages of a Grand Slam, and then you have to meet them. They always come up with their best tennis when it matters the most.

"But it's a process of learning, a process of developing and improving as a tennis player, as a person; and finding the way to mentally overcome those pressures and expectations and issues that you have. The mental approach has to be positive. You know, I have to win this match. There's no other way."

Novak admitted that both Federer and Nadal had spurred him to improve his own game. "They have made me a better player. Now it has turned around because I have started believing I can win. I lost my fear. I believed in my abilities more than ever."

Indeed, self-belief can be a tennis player's greatest weapon.

> They have made me a better player. Now it has turned around because I have started believing I can win. I lost my fear. I believed in my abilities more than ever.

Novak Djokovic

LEFT: Novak hits a forehand to Nadal on Centre Court in the 2011 Wimbledon final.

THE
DJOKER

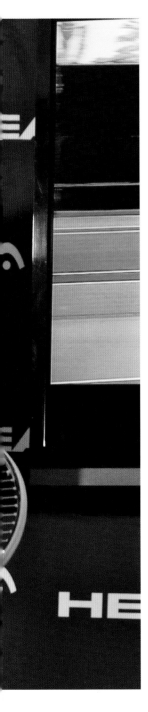

LEFT: Novak once filmed a TV advert for Head rackets in a Maria Sharapova-style wig.

For a long time he was known as "The Djoker", thanks to his very skilled impersonations of other players. It all started in the summer of 2007, during the grass-court season. While practising at The Queen's Club, in London – a famous warm-up tournament for Wimbledon – he decided to do impressions of some of the playing styles of his fellow players: their mannerisms, their idiosyncratic service actions, or their nervous tics. It was pretty harmless, good-natured stuff. There was Maria Sharapova's accentuated ball bounce, for example, and Rafa Nadal's vigorous underpants-tugging, and Andy Roddick's fiddling with his hat and shirt. He mimicked the likes of Goran Ivanišević, Lleyton Hewitt and Roger Federer, too.

Initially these funny skits were simply for the benefit of his coaching team. But that day at The Queen's Club, a BBC film crew happened to be beside the practice courts and Novak's antics were captured on film and then broadcast. They went viral online. Word quickly got around that Novak was quite the skilled impersonator.

By the time the tour had moved to New York for the US Open, Novak's mimicry was, among international fans, the best known of his characteristics. Journalists and commentators were regularly asking him to imitate his fellow players. Spectators, always keen to lighten up the rather sombre moods that fall over certain tennis matches, loved it. After Novak beat Carlos Moyá to reach the US Open semi-finals, the on-court interviewer Michael Barkann suggested he might do some impressions there and then, on the court. The resulting skits, which took off Sharapova and Nadal, had the entire crowd laughing and cheering. The images were beamed all over the world. Novak was no longer Djokovic; he was The Djoker.

"I enjoy it. I'm really happy that the people accept it in a positive way," he said in New York. "I'm not trying to make fun of Maria or Rafa or anybody else. Just trying to make the

people laugh and have a good time; trying to enjoy the tennis on the court and off the court as well."

He really made people laugh a few years later when he filmed a TV advert for Head rackets, donning a blonde wig and presenting a Sharapova impression worthy of an Oscar. "It makes me feel beautiful on the court, it makes me feel great," he said to camera in full camp mode. "It makes me feel a woman on the court. Hi, my name is Maria Sharapova and my game is instinct." After which he collapsed into fits of laughter.

But there was a downside to all this mickey-taking. Novak explained how fans were coming up to him and congratulating him more for his impersonations than for his actual tennis. "I was wondering, am I here for the impersonation, entertaining, or to play tennis?"

Behind all the fun and games, The Djoker had a serious point. Was there a risk his impressions would cause spectators (and, more importantly, opponents and potential sponsors) to think he wasn't serious about the business of winning tennis?

It all came to a head at the 2008 Australian Open when, in the middle of a match, a fan called out, asking Novak to do a Sharapova impression. Right then,

OPPOSITE: Hosting the first semi-final of the 2008 Eurovision Song Contest in Belgrade.

RIGHT: Novak impersonates Brazilian tennis player Gustavo Kuerten.

he realised he was becoming more renowned for his comic side-show than for his actual tennis. There was a further problem in that certain players started resenting the way he was mimicking them. So he decided to rein back on the skits. "I wasn't trying to offend anybody," he said at the time.

Just a few days later he beat Jo-Wilfried Tsonga to win his first Grand Slam. The Djoker was no more. From now on it was serious Novak.

Well, not that serious. In May 2008 he appeared as a guest at one of the Eurovision Song Contest semi-finals in Belgrade, and joined in a tribute song to his capital city, originally recorded by the legendary, and since deceased, Serbian rock singer Đorđe Marjanović.

The Serb's playful character comes across in other ways, too. In 2010, he acted in a music video for a song called "Hello", by French DJ and producer Martin Solveig and Canadian pop band Dragonette. The song itself was hugely successful, going platinum in terms of sales and reaching the top spot in one of the United States' dance charts, as well as number one in the main charts of several European countries. It was featured in several very popular TV series, as well as adverts, a video game and a feature film.

The video for the song was filmed at Roland Garros in Paris, just before the start of the real 2010 French Open. It features a match between Solveig and fellow superstar DJ Bob Sinclar on one of Roland Garros's stadium courts. Novak himself makes only a cameo appearance, but it's a crucial one: at the end of the match he marches on court to remonstrate with the umpire over a line call that had gone against Solveig, so frustrated that he even shakes the umpire's chair back and forth.

Although he appears for only a few seconds, his acting ability – coupled with his fame as an impersonator – obviously gained him some notoriety within the movie industry. The following year he was invited to play himself in a very high-budget Hollywood action film starring Sylvester Stallone, Bruce Willis, Chuck Norris and Jean-Claude Van Damme, called The Expendables 2.

In a warehouse in the Bulgarian capital Sofia, he filmed several scenes, at one point fighting off baddies with his tennis racket. It seems Novak was more expendable than he thought, however. In the final version of the movie, his scenes were cut out.

Novak has had more luck in the world of natural science. In 2021 he had a species of mollusc named after him. Balkan scientists were on a field trip near Podgorica, the capital of Montenegro, when they stumbled upon a new species of aquatic snail with a milky-white shell in the shape of an elongated cone, which had evolved to live in caves beneath a Balkan mountain range. Now called *Travunijana djokovici*, the creature is small, very rare and likes nothing better than sliding around in the mud.

But why did the scientists name it after Novak? "To discover some of the world's rarest animals that inhabit the unique underground habitats, to reach inaccessible cave and spring habitats, and for the restless work during processing of the collected material, you need Novak's energy and enthusiasm," the researchers explain.

It seems scientists and tiny creatures have a natural affinity for Novak. In 2022, a researcher at the University of Belgrade announced that a new species of Serbian beetle was to be named after the country's most famous sporting celebrity. Discovered in an underground pit in eastern Serbia, it now goes by the name of *Duvalius djokovici*, due to its strength, speed, flexibility, durability and survival skills in a treacherous environment. "He is the man who did much for this country," the researcher enthused. "We feel urged to pay him back in the way we can."

Invertebrates are all very well. But to discover Novak's true personality, we need to examine the people closest to him. Closest of all is his wife.

Jelena Ristić, like her husband, was born and brought up in Belgrade. Her father is Miomir, her mother Vera, and her older sister Marija.

Jelena and Novak were teenage sweethearts. Although they first met when they were still at high school in the late 1990s, it wasn't until 2005 that they started dating, when he was making his initial forays on the ATP tour and she was studying business at Bocconi University in Milan. The bonds between them must have been strong, as Novak managed to keep the relationship alive, even while he was criss-crossing the globe in pursuit of prize money and ranking points.

"Us getting together was like science fiction, almost," Jelena said in an interview with *Hello!* magazine. "I was a student barely getting by, and he was a very young tennis player who also had no money to spare on expensive trips. Aeroplanes were, at the time, something utterly out of our reach. We contrived and devised these plans how to meet, how to make our relationship work."

Once Jelena had completed her studies in Milan, graduating with a degree in business administration and management, the couple moved in together at Novak's residence in Monte Carlo. Here she continued studying, this time at the International University of Monaco where, by 2011, she had completed a

master's degree in luxury goods and services. Her final thesis analysed the importance of social media for fashion brands.

In 2013 Novak finally proposed to Jelena. The method of proposal was like something out of a Hollywood romantic comedy. Novak suggested to his girlfriend that they go on an early-morning hot-air balloon ride. Secretly, he had arranged for a second hot-air balloon that would unfurl a giant banner with the words "Will you marry me?" writ large upon it. Unfortunately not everything went to plan. While the pilot struggled to unfurl the banner mid-air, his balloon accidentally caught fire, causing the balloon to descend rapidly. Jelena said she thought the words on the banner were a commercial message, and she couldn't fathom why on earth someone would be advertising to an empty sky at seven o'clock in the morning. Then she turned round and noticed Novak was down on one knee in the basket, with a ring in his hand. Their fate was sealed.

ABOVE: Jelena pregnant with the couple's first child at the 2014 Wimbledon championships.

RIGHT: Jelena and son Stefan watch Novak in the 2018 Wimbledon final.

It wasn't long before Jelena fell pregnant. By the time the 2014 Wimbledon championships came round, her bump was very prominent indeed.

"The date is coming closer. The stomach is growing," Novak revealed after one of his match wins that year at the All England Club. "For us, it's a new chapter of our lives. It's a new experience. We're full of joy. What can I say? It can only bring positive things to us. It's the most beautiful news that I ever received when she told me she was pregnant. This is the crown of our relationship."

Imminent fatherhood proved to be no distraction as Novak won his second Wimbledon title that summer, beating Roger Federer in the final.

Just days after his triumph, he and Jelena were in Montenegro – in a town called Sveti Stefan – to get married. The ceremony itself was in the church of St Stephen, while the reception took place at a luxury resort called Aman Sveti Stefan.

SINGLES SERVICE AND RETURN RECORD

	2006	2011	2015
Singles Service Record			
Aces	285	343	471
Double Faults	154	143	135
1st Serve In	63%	65%	66%
1st Serve Points Won	72%	74%	74%
2nd Serve Points Won	53%	56%	60%
Break Points Faced	330	351	358
Break Points Saved	63%	65%	68%
Service Games Played	652	899	1,082
Service Games Won	81%	86%	89%
Total Service Points Won	65%	68%	70%
Singles Return Record			
1st Serve Return Points Won	30%	36%	34%
2nd Serve Return Points Won	51%	58%	57%
Break Points Opportunities	371	692	824
Break Points Converted	45%	48%	44%
Return Games Played	634	860	1,057
Return Games Won	26%	39%	34%
Return Points Won	39%	45%	43%
Total Points Won	52%	56%	56%

2018	2022	2006 – 2022 Comparison					Career
342	291						6,750
152	92						2,776
66%	66%						65%
74%	77%						74%
57%	56%						55%
301	205						6,141
65%	64%						65%
830	602						15,128
87%	88%						86%
68%	70%						67%
34%	33%						34%
55%	56%						55%
617	388						10,634
40%	43%						44%
813	576						14,699
30%	29%						32%
42%	41%						42%
55%	55%						55%

Halfway down the small country's Adriatic coast, it's a pretty special place. The resort comprises a large villa overlooking the beach, called Villa Milocer, and then a tiny islet, just over 200 metres long and dotted with orange-roofed cottages, is connected to the mainland by a thin strip of beach. Among the guests at the three-day ceremony were fellow Serbian players Janko Tipsarević, Viktor Troicki and Nenad Zimonjić, as well as Novak's coach at the time, Boris Becker.

Like many celebrity couples, they sold their wedding photos and interview to *Hello!* magazine, with the sizeable fee going to the Novak Djokovic Foundation.

"Seeing her for the first time in her wedding dress, smiling and walking towards me ... She looked like an angel," Novak said in the interview. "I was trying to be present in that moment and memorise it. I was focused on her, and her smile, and our baby. It really was a perfect moment."

Jelena added: "The wedding was everything we hoped it would be. Our family and closest friends united in a beautiful setting in celebration of our love. It was truly emotional and unforgettable for us."

She admitted to being very nervous. "Everything seemed a blur. I was seeing him through tears and immediately started crying when I saw him. I was just so happy and probably being pregnant makes it quite difficult to control the emotions. I am so blessed to have him in my life. I couldn't ask for a better partner than him."

OPPOSITE: Wife Jelena speaks on stage at the Novak Djokovic Foundation New York dinner in 2013.

RIGHT: With the trophy at the 2015 US Open.

Three months later, on October 22nd, the couple's son Stefan was born. While parenthood might be a distraction to most fathers with busy, demanding careers, for Novak it had the opposite effect. Within a week of the birth he was in the French capital at the Paris Masters, where he galloped through to victory without dropping a set. Then on to the ATP World Tour Finals in London, where he demolished Marin Čilić, Stan Wawrinka and Tomáš Berdych, and took out Kei Nishikori in three sets. He didn't have to contest the final as Roger Federer was forced to drop out with a back injury.

The 2015 season started equally brilliantly, with tournament victories at the Australian Open, the Masters events in Indian Wells, Miami, Monte Carlo and Rome, followed in the summer by finishing runner-up at Roland Garros and triumphing at Wimbledon and the US Open. He seemed unstoppable.

"I can say definitely that it's the best, most joyful thing that ever has happened to me and my wife," he said during that year's Australian Open. "We are so blessed and grateful to have a child. He's a little angel."

Although he didn't travel with his wife and newborn that year, he said technology allowed him to keep in touch. "It helps me to stay connected and see them and watch them on a daily basis. I can't wait to be with them. Everything that you do as a father is very special. Everything that you see, all the facial expressions, changes on a weekly basis, daily basis, as a matter of fact, is quite

remarkable. It's inexplicable for somebody that hasn't experienced it before. I'm completely fulfilled in every aspect of my life. That gives a whole another meaning and purpose to my tennis as well. I'm trying to draw that energy and motivation and love that I have for my family and for my boy into the tennis court as well."

By 2016, things weren't nearly as rosy in the Djokovic household. In March that year Novak was photographed on a dinner date with a famous Indian actress called Deepika Padukone, at a Los Angeles restaurant. He had met the Bollywood star the previous year at a tennis event called the International Premier Tennis League.

Understandably, given the renown of both Novak and Deepika, the gossip media went into overdrive. How much the incident directly affected Novak's tennis, we'll never really know. However, later that year his game nose-dived. At Wimbledon, he suffered an inexplicable loss in the third round to Sam Querrey, an American ranked around 40 in the world at that time. It was his earliest exit in a Grand Slam since 2009.

It turned out that the evening before, Jelena had suddenly left Wimbledon, heading straight for the airport with the couple's son. She then went on holiday alone in South Africa while Novak looked after Stefan at home in Monte Carlo.

"It was nothing physical. It's not an injury," he said of the surprising Wimbledon result. "It was some other things that I was going through privately. We all have private issues and things that are more challenges than issues, more things that we have to encounter and overcome in order to evolve as a human being."

While that answer may sound rather cryptic, he was more revealing in a later podcast interview called "In Depth with Graham Bensinger". There he tried to explain his cataclysmic two-year drop in form (well, cataclysmic by his standards) after his Roland Garros win in 2016, which eventually saw his world ranking drop from number one down to 22.

"I realised that I came to the stage of my life and career where I had to dig deeper and understand myself on a much deeper level than I had until that point," he said. "I put a lot of weight ... on winning the French Open and completing the four Slams. I think I put way too much weight on that. The happiness would be dependent on me winning or not. Then I realised when I won, I was not fulfilled fully; something was lacking. Was there some dark place where there was some little child hidden in the corner, crying and asking for attention?"

He admitted that tennis and his constant obsession with victory had caused him to ignore his emotional wellbeing. "I left that inner child aside and he didn't grow with me," he added. "I didn't grow up emotionally as much as I did tennis-wise."

He also admitted how much the difficulties in his marriage had affected him. "I learned that when you expect the least, that's when life will give you something to work at internally. I realised up to that moment the relationships with the closest people in my life were quite superficial and shallow because I didn't know how to handle that."

Bensinger asked him what it taught him about his marriage to Jelena. "It taught me that we have to go on this journey together, and it's inevitable that she has to endure the same journey as I do, at the same time, otherwise we can't stay together. I'm really grateful and happy that she embarked on the same journey – her own journey – but in parallel, at the same time as I did."

Wherever this parallel journey took Novak and Jelena, it worked. Results improved and in the summer of 2018 he won both Wimbledon and the US Open, and was back in the world top ten. The September before, Novak and Jelena were celebrating the birth of their daughter Tara.

Nowadays, much of Jelena's energy is directed into Novak's charity, the Novak Djokovic Foundation, where she works as director. "It is focused on empowering families and future leaders of the society by investing in quality early-childhood education and development," she explains on her personal website. The foundation work includes building and operating kindergartens across Serbia for children aged up to eight years old. They train teachers, run support groups for parents and invest in research on child development.

In an interview with an American magazine called *Leaders*, she explained her and Novak's motivation for the foundation. "Novak and I grew up in a war-torn country in difficult circumstances. However, we were fortunate to grow up in families that nurtured education and understood the value of early-childhood development. For us, it was only natural that we do the same through the work of our foundation."

Jelena is keen to get across the message that her husband wants to help young people in particular. "He always stresses how lucky he was to have the care, love and support from an early age from his family, and how much their belief in him and his dreams meant to his success. This is why now, through our foundation, he is able to do just that: provide this support system so that other children like him can dare to dream."

Jelena is also involved in a magazine aimed at students called *Original Magazin*, which covers culture, education, the arts, sport and science.

Married to one of the most famous sportsmen on the planet, she clearly needs to be careful about what she says in public. Interviews with her are rare. Even her personal website jelenadjokovic.com does not look like it is regularly updated. One passage on the website gives an intriguing insight into her personality, however:

"I would like to be remembered as a curious soul who loves life and lifelong learning," she writes. "The roles I take on in this life are helping me grow in so many ways, and my biggest and most important teachers in life are my children. They have reconnected me with my true self, helped me unveil my soul, and showed me how to lead a more meaningful life.

"I live by values of gratitude, honesty, respect, kindness, forgiveness, and love, and try to practise them through everything I do. One of the hardest lessons I hope to learn and practise every day in my life is how to love myself fully. Everything I absorb through my learning helps me evolve and grow. I tend to make mistakes a lot, that is my process of learning."

> He [Djokovic] always stresses how lucky he was to have the care, love and support from an early age from his family, and how much their belief in him and his dreams meant to his success. This is why now, through our foundation, he is able to do just that: provide this support system so that other children like him can dare to dream.

Jelena Djokovic

LEFT: Novak, wife Jelena, mother Dijana and father Srdjan attend the Novak Djokovic Foundation party in London in 2013.

THE MATCH

US OPEN
September 12th 2011

USTA Billie Jean King National Tennis Center, New York City, USA

Final: Novak Djokovic beat Rafael Nadal 6–2, 6–4, 6–7, 6–1

The year 2011 was Novak's *annus mirabilis*, and of all his matches that year, the US Open final against Rafa Nadal was arguably the most mirabilis of all.

His record so far that season was incredible – some say it was the greatest season ever recorded by a male tennis player. He'd already won nine tournaments in 2011: the Australian Open, Wimbledon, five Masters events, one ATP 500 and one ATP 250. So when he arrived in New York City, as the number-one player in the world, he was favourite to take the title.

His first two rounds, against lowly ranked players, were embarrassingly easy. In the first, his Irish opponent was forced to retire, while in the second, he came very close to dispatching an Argentinian player with a triple bagel. In rounds three and four, Russia's Nikolay Davydenko and Ukraine's Alexandr Dolgopolov barely resisted. In fact, it wasn't until the quarter finals, against fellow Serb Janko Tipsarević, that he actually lost a set.

His semi-final against Roger Federer was a different matter altogether, requiring five hard-fought sets over almost four hours.

It wasn't just each other the players had to combat during that fortnight in New York. The elements, too, provided a significant challenge. As the tournament had been getting underway, an earthquake had struck the eastern seaboard of the United States, requiring officials to undertake structural checks on many of the stands at the Billie Jean King National Tennis Center.

The weather was frightful, too, with the remnants of Hurricane Irene whipping up storms. By the end of the fortnight, heavy rain would push the men's final from the scheduled Sunday to the following Monday.

By then, Novak knew his opponent would be the mighty Rafa Nadal. From the very start, the level of tennis from both players was astounding. The Spaniard started strongly, breaking serve to take a 2–0 lead, while Novak quickly regrouped, winning six consecutive games to secure the first set. At times, the roaring crowd in the Arthur Ashe Stadium were treated to rallies lasting 20 or more shots, sometimes even 30 or more. While Nadal attempted to blast his opponent off the court, Novak regularly contorted and stretched his arms and legs into seemingly impossible positions in his efforts to retrieve the ball. The Spaniard was bamboozled; the spectators could barely believe their eyes. Even Novak himself seemed surprised at his own athleticism.

The most scintillating game of the match was without doubt the third of the second set – a 17-minute duel with Nadal serving, in which he was pulled, kicking and groaning, into eight deuce points. On the sixth break point, at the end of yet another long, back-breaking rally, Novak finally won the game when the Mallorcan placed a weak smash into the net.

Then followed a duel of epic proportions, the scoreline seesawing frustratingly between each player. On more than a few occasions, the chair umpire Carlos Ramos had to demand quiet from supporters in both camps who were rudely calling out, either during serve or in the middle of crucial rallies. Novak seemed more rattled by the interruptions than Nadal.

BELOW: Some rallies during the match comprised more than 30 shots.

At 6–5 in the third set, Novak found himself serving for the match. So imagine the noise echoing round the stadium when Nadal fought back and won the tiebreak. Everyone at Flushing Meadows that day knew they were witnessing a historical battle, and they definitely wanted more.

Finally, after four hours and ten minutes, the Serbian player served out the fourth set 6–1 to secure the title. He let himself fall backwards onto the court, before turning towards his celebrating team, letting out a roar, dropping to his knees and kissing the court.

"If this were a fight, Nadal would have been punched to a pulp at the end but Djokovic's knuckles would have been bruised beyond recognition," wrote *The Guardian* newspaper's tennis correspondent Kevin Mitchell.

Shortly after his victory, the Serb admitted to feeling "emotionally and physically and mentally drained". And he talked of his long journey to the top of the sport. "I know this couldn't come overnight. It's a long process," he said. "Throughout all my life I've been working, being committed to this sport 100 per cent. That's the only the way you can really succeed: the right balance between private life and life on tour, which is very requiring, demanding."

He talked of the episodes in his past that had enabled him to become, in 2011, indisputably the greatest player on the planet. "I go back in my thoughts, in my childhood, all these memories growing up, playing tennis, spending time in Serbia. That helped me to become a better person, to appreciate things in life more.

"I owe my parents a lot, because I think they have done a great job in bringing me up and supporting me throughout all my career. This is individual sport, but it's not an effort of myself. I may be on the court by myself winning or losing, I maybe take the whole credit or all the blame, but it's actually the team, the family, the support, everybody around you that spends their energy as well. All my team members, they go through this with me and they put their energy and effort into my success."

"This is individual sport, but it's not an effort of myself. I may be on the court by myself winning or losing, I maybe take the whole credit or all the blame, but it's actually the team, the family, the support, everybody around you that spends their energy as well.

Novak Djokovic

LEFT: Novak and Nadal treated the crowd to four sets of incredible tennis.

6

NOVAK THE BUSINESSMAN

US

LEFT: Novak receives the winner's prize cheque for the Rogers Cup ATP Masters Series in Montreal in 2007.

Since he first started playing professional tennis, back in 2003, in prize money alone Novak has earned over US$175 million, more than any other player in history ... by a country mile. His nearest rivals, Rafa Nadal and Roger Federer, have amassed $135 million and $131 million respectively in on-court earnings. No one else comes close.

It's by sheer dint of hard work. Novak's 24 Grand Slam singles titles (and counting), plus his 39 Masters titles, and 33 additional tournament wins ensure the pay cheques keep rolling in.

On the ATP tour and across the Grand Slams, prize money is more generous now than it's ever been. In 2023, the ATP tour increased its total prize fund to $217.9 million. Three of the Grand Slams currently pay their male and female singles winners in excess of $2 million each, while the Australian Open pays just a smidge below this amount.

But when it comes to globally famous players such as Novak, Rafa Nadal, and the recently retired Roger Federer, prize money is mere pocket change in comparison to the eye-watering amounts they can earn in sponsorship money.

How much sportsmen and women earn is not an exact science. It's not as if they publish their tax returns for the world to see. There is one research body, though, that attempts to keep tabs on these figures. Every year, American business magazine *Forbes* publishes a list of the world's 50 highest-paid athletes across all sports, using research from industry insiders on prize money, salaries, bonuses, sponsorship deals, appearance fees, licensing income and business ventures. The 2023 list ranks Portuguese soccer legend Cristiano Ronaldo at the top, with total annual earnings of $136 million. Fellow footballers Lionel Messi and Kylian Mbappé come second and third, with $130 million and $120 million respectively.

Interestingly, because of his decision to forego the Covid vaccine (see Chapter 8), and his resulting loss of certain

ABOVE: Novak lost Peugeot as a sponsor following his Covid vaccine debacle.

LEFT: Novak attending "A Conversation with Novak Djokovic" at the ASICS 5th Avenue flagship store in New York

OPPOSITE TOP: Launching Uniqlo 2013 Wimbledon Matchwear.

OPPOSITE BOTTOM: Lacoste, with its famous crocodile logo, is Novak's shirt sponsor.

sponsors, as well as exclusions from the 2022 Australian Open and US Open, Novak didn't feature on the 2022 or 2023 *Forbes* top 50 athlete rich list. But in previous years, thanks to handsome deals with the likes of Seiko watches, and car brands Peugeot and Mercedes-Benz, he has been a regular contender.

According to *Forbes*, in 2022 Novak earned a total of $27.1 million – $7.1 million on the court and $20 million off it. Because of more lucrative sponsorship deals (and crucially because they agreed to have Covid vaccines), Roger Federer, Naomi Osaka, Serena Williams and Rafa Nadal all earned more than this.

Due to his refusal to be vaccinated, the Serb may have lost several sponsors – including Peugeot and software firm Ultimate Kronos Group – but he is still supported financially by plenty of blue-chip companies. Lacoste is his clothing brand, paying him a reported $8 million a year. Although there were rumours they almost dropped their star player because of the Covid debacle, in the end they stuck with him. He is currently in a contract until 2025. Lacoste plan to release an annual clothing collection in his name.

"As their global ambassador, I am important to them," Novak said in 2022 when other sponsors were distancing themselves from him. "But their position was not easy. They have told us that they have been under pressure from the media, from some clients that maybe weren't happy with me staying with the company.

"Challenges always present themselves, so to say, but I think they made a good choice and I am grateful. I will try to represent the Lacoste brand just like I did up until now in the best possible way. After all, it is a brand with great tradition – one of the greatest in tennis. And I am proud to wear the crocodile on my shirt." In previous years his clothing sponsors had included Adidas, Sergio Tacchini and Uniqlo.

His shoe brand is ASICS, while for rackets it's Head. Contract details are sketchy, but some media outlets have reported the deals to be worth $4 million a year and $7.5 million a year respectively. In addition, he has deals with Austrian drinks brand Waterdrop, Austrian banking group Raiffeisen and Swiss watchmaker Hublot.

"Novak Djokovic is his own person," said the latter when asked whether they supported his decision to forego the vaccine. "We cannot comment on any of his personal decisions."

The agreement with Waterdrop, a start-up company which prides itself on not using plastic bottles, is more of an investment for Novak, rather than a high-earning sponsorship deal. The company calls him "an investor and ambassador".

PRIZE MONEY

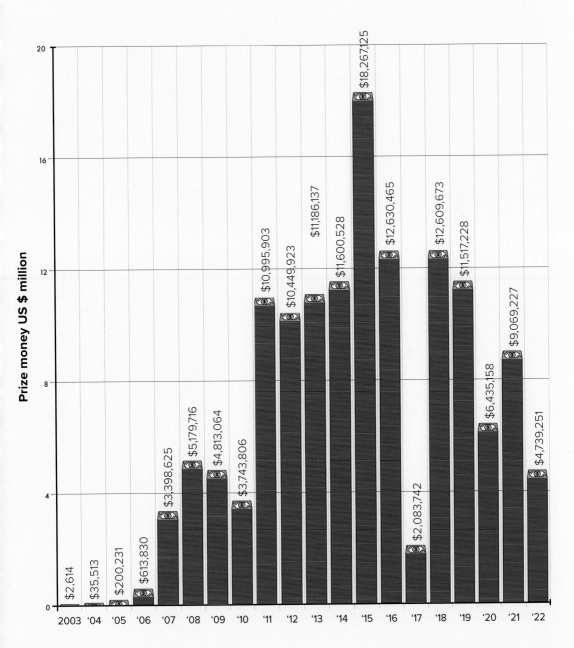

Prize money US $ million

- 2003 — $2,614
- '04 — $35,513
- '05 — $200,231
- '06 — $613,830
- '07 — $3,398,625
- '08 — $5,179,716
- '09 — $4,813,064
- '10 — $3,743,806
- '11 — $10,995,903
- '12 — $10,449,923
- '13 — $11,186,137
- '14 — $11,600,528
- '15 — $18,267,125
- '16 — $12,630,465
- '17 — $2,083,742
- '18 — $12,609,673
- '19 — $11,517,228
- '20 — $6,435,158
- '21 — $9,069,227
- '22 — $4,739,251

There have been reports that he made a "significant seven-figure investment".

"Determined to raise awareness about the negative impact of unhealthy sugary drinks in plastic bottles – now, we're not alone in our vision," they state on their website. "Novak Djokovic shares our sentiment for change and, with his unique experience, is now supporting Waterdrop to make an even bigger impact."

Novak supports the drive to rid sport of plastic water bottles. "A healthy lifestyle includes proper hydration with no concessions on environmental impact," he says of the brand. "I believe that by working together, we can make a real difference and get rid of all the plastic bottles on the tour."

The Serbian player is involved in more than a few business ventures. Much of this is conducted through the Djokovic family's company Family Sport, which prides itself on being a "socially responsible company by raising awareness of the importance of sport", and fostering "values that characterise a harmonious and successful family". Founded in December 2005, and based in Belgrade, its main ventures consist of the Novak-branded restaurant group and the Novak Tennis Center, also in Belgrade.

Currently Family Sport has three Novak Cafe & Restaurants – two in Belgrade and one in the northern Serbian city of Novi Sad. The marketing video for the cafe-restaurants couldn't be cheesier. "The restaurants of the world's best player, Novak Djokovic, attract people with charming and pleasant atmosphere," boasts a promotional film on the website. "International gastronomic specialties with an exquisite combination of different flavours, authentically designed interior and top-class service make the restaurant unique and favourite among all generations." Diners won't be surprised to find a substantial offering of gluten-free dishes on the menu. Family Sport is currently looking to franchise its restaurant brand in other countries.

Novak used to own a vegan, gluten-free restaurant in

LEFT: Novak's deal with Head is reportedly worth $7.5 million a year.

ABOVE: The Djokovic family restaurant "Novak" in Belgrade.

Monaco called Eqvita. It opened in 2016 but, perhaps rather naïvely, the player failed to take into account the almost universal distaste of veganism among French diners. Unfortunately Eqvita was reported closed in 2019.

The Novak Tennis Center is far more successful. Sitting right on the banks of the River Danube, in central Belgrade, it features 11 Roland Garros-style clay courts and three DecoTurf hard courts (the type used at the US Open), as well as gym and fitness facilities, physiotherapy, a children's playground, a player's lounge and a restaurant. Top-level coaching is offered to young players there, and Novak's good friend and former Davis Cup teammate Viktor Troicki was formerly head coach. Much of the day-to-day operations here are carried out by Novak's father Srdjan and uncle Goran.

"The Novak Tennis Center's mission and vision are to provide a holistic approach to the preparation and development of young athletes," says the marketing blurb on the website. "We prioritise both the training process and the educational aspects, as well as the cultivation of values within each individual athlete. At the core of our approach and methods lies a commitment to life values, a strong willpower, and an unwavering drive for personal growth and progress in all aspects of life. End goal? The development of our athletes into satisfied and accomplished personalities, both on a professional and personal level."

In 2023, Novak and his family returned the land and facilities of the Novak Tennis Center to the city of Belgrade.

The Djokovic family also owns a vineyard and wine production business in Serbia's central Šumadija region. According to trade magazine *The Drinks Business*, it's a five-hectare vineyard with a projected capacity for 60,000 litres of wine a year. The first vines were planted in 2016 and by 2020 around 8,500 bottles had gone on sale in Serbia, under two labels – Djokovic Syrah 2020 and Djokovic Chardonnay 2020.

According to the Serbian wine magazine *Vino & Fino*, the chardonnay offers hints of melon, pear and mango, with tropical notes in the finish, along with baked lemon, creamy tones of butter and the juiciness of ripe fruit. The syrah, meanwhile, has a meaty aroma of black fruit and wet stone, with floral tones, spices and wood. It's moderately full, fleshy and persistent, slightly spicy and mineral, with velvety tannins.

Always conscious of his healthy image, Novak has distanced himself somewhat from the brand, although he did attend the launch. Uncle Goran offered the following comparison between wine and nephew: "There are many challenges, but we try to achieve the maximum in this business, as in everything," he said in *Vino & Fino*. "Even Novak's racket is not perfect, but he is still the best in the world."

One of Novak's more intriguing investments is an 80 per cent stake in a Danish biotechnology firm called QuantBioRes, which claims to be developing a non-vaccine treatment for Covid-19. This involves a peptide that the company claims "is able to inhibit infection with COVID-19 virus with up to 96 per cent efficiency".

Like many of the world's top players, Novak has invested handsomely in property. His principal residence, clearly for tax reasons, is his apartment in Monaco. According to *The Washington Post*, in 2017 he bought a pair of condominium apartments in the SoHo district of New York City, for $10 million. Two years later a three-bedroom condominium in Miami was added to his portfolio. According to Realtor.com, this property sits in a development designed by Italian architect Renzo Piano, called Eighty Seven Park. No one is sure how much he paid but if you consider that the building's penthouse was on the market for $68 million, that gives you an idea of the quality of the real estate.

"I simply love the design of this building," Djokovic said in a press statement. "This is an unexpected location in a neighborhood that's rapidly growing, and that's what attracted me to buy here. It will be my new retreat."

"With the curved prow of an ocean liner, the beachfront condominium provides unobstructed views of the Atlantic Ocean," writes Claudine Zap on Realtor.com. "Designed with an open layout, the luxury residence boasts 10-foot ceilings, floor-to-ceiling windows, and a wraparound balcony. The eco-conscious structure is the only one in Miami that offers residents a key to a private, gated park. As an added bonus, a botanist on the building's staff can also help owners with their personal terrace gardens. Other amenities include a spa with Turkish hammam, a fitness centre, and two ocean-front pools. Residents can unwind at the wine bar or refuel at the outdoor juice bar."

By the time you read this, Novak's business empire is sure to have expanded further. The closer he gets to retiring from tennis, the more he will focus on his commercial interests.

OPPOSITE: With friend and former head coach at the Novak Tennis Center Viktor Troicki.

THE MATCH

AUSTRALIAN OPEN

January 29th/30th 2012

Melbourne Park, Melbourne, Australia

Final: Novak Djokovic beat Rafael Nadal 5–7, 6–4, 6–2, 6–7, 7–5

It was the longest Grand Slam final of all time, enduring for a muscle- and brain-sapping 5 hours and 53 minutes. When Novak took on Rafa Nadal in the final of the 2012 Australian Open, everyone expected sparks to fly. They just didn't expect them to fly for quite so long.

"Both of us, physically, we took the last drop of energy that we had from our bodies," Novak said once he'd recovered from his ordeal.

Although the Serb was the eventual winner, the match started badly for him. In the third game of the first set he rolled his ankle slightly, while his right shoulder appeared to be moving stiffly. Then, at 2–2, facing breakpoint, he sent an errant forehand a few inches beyond Nadal's baseline. Fuming, he marched to his chair for the changeover, threw his racket to the ground in disgust, pulled off his white shirt – already damp from the muggy Melbourne heat – and replaced it with a black one. There had been suspicions that Novak's energy levels were already depleted after his 4 hours and 50 minutes-long semi-final against Andy Murray in the previous round. It looked like there might not be enough fuel left in the tank.

That first set was riddled with unforced errors, 19 of them from Novak, making for a disappointing spectacle. But by set number two, both players seemed to have found their stride. The Serb cranked up his power and his mental game, breaking the Spaniard to go 4–1 up, punishing him on the returns of serve, and taking the second set 6–4.

It was a similar story in the third set, with Novak again dictating play. Nadal's head dropped in despair as yet another blistering forehand zipped past him to lose him the third set, after 45 minutes.

By the time of the fourth set, however, both players were performing at the very peak of their ability, neither one willing to succumb on a single point. The Mallorcan battled furiously to save three break points and level the set at 4–4. His groundstrokes looked riskier, skimming the court boundaries both wide and deep. Novak was stretched to his limit but defended admirably – all this despite it being plainly obvious that the vast majority of the vociferous crowd were siding with his Spanish opponent.

Not long before midnight, rain clouds appeared in the Melbourne skies, and the players left the court for a short period as the roof rolled across from above. Once back in play, it was Nadal who looked the stronger player. Sure enough, with the tiebreak underway, he raced to a lead, taking it 7–2.

So this match of attrition ground on into the wee hours of the Monday morning. In the fifth set, Nadal broke to go 4–2 up, and then Novak broke back to level again.

BELOW: Novak's battle with Nadal in 2012 is the longest Grand Slam final of all time.

Then followed one of those rare points of sheer brilliance you wish might never end: 32 strokes in all, after which Novak sent the ball long and collapsed onto his back. The entire crowd in Rod Laver Arena (including Rod Laver himself) rose as one to applaud both combatants. While most spectators were rooting for Nadal, they clearly offered just as much respect to Novak.

ABOVE: Novak
revels in his
historic victory.

OPPOSITE TOP LEFT:
Nadal celebrates
winning the
fourth set.

**OPPOSITE TOP
RIGHT:** Novak
removes his
sweat-soaked
shirt after winning
match point.

OPPOSITE BOTTOM:
Novak and
Nadal taking a
well-deserved seat
during the
presentation
and speeches.

The body language of the Spaniard suggested he believed victory was in sight. Nevertheless, he had to fight through a break point to hold his serve.

Finally, Novak found himself serving for the match. After an errant smash and a weak backhand return, he had to defend break point himself. Then came a strong serve, after which he counter-attacked his opponent's return. Suddenly the long match was over. Novak removed his sweat-soaked shirt and went straight to his support team at the side of the court. They embraced him. And he deserved it.

Incredibly, given the effort both players had given, they still had to wait on the court while the presentation and sponsors' speeches droned on. Fortunately they were allowed to sit down throughout.

Shortly afterwards, it was pointed out to Novak that the match had broken the record for the longest ever Grand Slam final. "Just to hear that fact is making me cry," he said. "I'm very proud to be part of this history."

Although he admitted that enduring such a long match had been painful, he said there was a pleasurable side to it, too. "You are in pain, you are suffering, you know that you're trying to activate your legs, you're trying to push yourself another point; just one more point, one more game. You're going through so much suffering, your toes are bleeding. Everything is just outrageous, you know, but you're still enjoying that pain."

The words of a true champion.

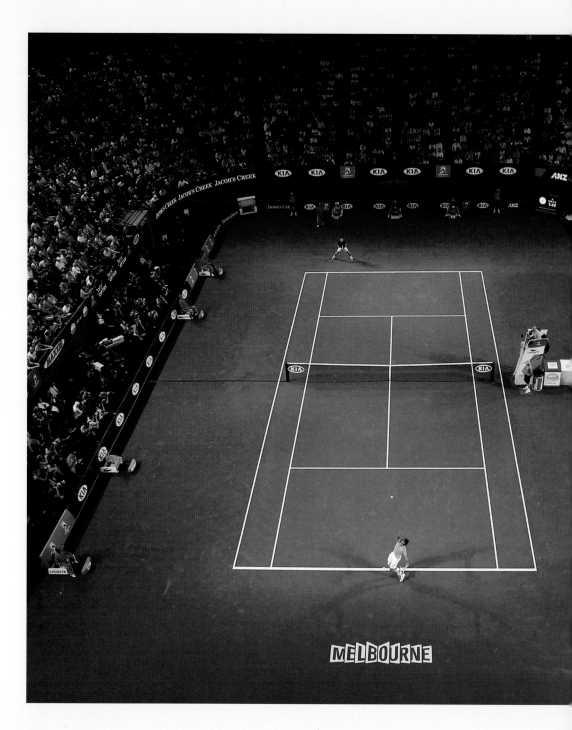

“You are in pain, you are suffering, you know that you're trying to activate your legs, you're trying to push yourself another point; just one more point, one more game ... Everything is just outrageous, you know, but you're still enjoying that pain.”

Novak Djokovic

LEFT: The crowd offered huge respect to both players during the match.

THE UNIVERSE ACCORDING TO NOVAK

LEFT: Novak was forced to retire from his second round match in the 2005 French Open.

Back in the 1980s, Martina Navratilova was the first tennis player to realise that what you did off the court was just as important, if not more important, than what you did on the court. On her way to winning 59 Grand Slam singles, doubles and mixed-doubles titles, she took fitness and diet to a new level, even at times bringing her own personal chef on the tour with her. Asked how dedicated she was to her sport, she once gave the following answer: "It's like ham and eggs: the chicken's involved, but the pig's committed."

Years later, reminded of this comment in an interview with *Men's Health* magazine, she then assessed Novak's commitment to his trade. "Novak's a pig, all right," she said. "He understands what to do: sleep, food, drink. It's all as important as tennis. And Novak is head and shoulders above the rest, the way he lives that attitude. He's a pro's pro. Perhaps that's why he doesn't get quite as much love as he should."

Novak really does take a holistic approach to his overall health. His vegan, gluten-free diet, his fitness, his embrace of Oriental medicine, his eschewal of Western medicine, his spiritualism, his mistrust of vaccines ... In a previous era, some might have called him "a bit of a hippie".

But there's a reason behind this unconventional attitude. When Novak was still a teenager, just starting out on the ATP tour, he often struggled at key stages in matches with breathing difficulties. "The Curse", he called it. "There was something about me that was broken, unhealthy, unfit," he wrote in his 2013 autobiography *Serve to Win*. "Some called it allergies, some called it asthma, some just called it being out of shape. But no matter what we called it, no one knew how to fix it."

The breathing problems were so bad that on several occasions he was forced to abandon matches: in 2005, for example, while competing for the first time at Roland Garros. The same year, in his first US Open match, against

Frenchman Gaël Monfils, he succumbed to four medical time-outs, at one point collapsing on the court and labouring to breathe. Even though he won the match, he was booed from the stadium, the spectators assuming his ailments were faked and all designed to put his opponent off his stride.

Novak suspected he simply wasn't fit enough and embarked on a gruelling regime, changing coaches and fitness trainers, in an effort to boost his physical power and technique. He meditated and took up yoga. He even underwent nasal surgery in order to ease his breathing.

There was an improvement. By January 2008 he had secured his first Grand Slam at the Australian Open. But among his fellow players he had gained a reputation for gamesmanship by – as they saw it – unnecessarily calling for the trainer during matches. At the 2008 US Open, the American player Andy Roddick mocked Novak, jokingly listing all his possible multiple ailments. "Both ankles, back, hip, cramp," he suggested. "Bird flu, anthrax, SARS, common cough and cold. He's either quick to call a trainer or he's the most courageous guy of all time."

None of this helped poor Novak. By late 2009 he decided to relocate his inter-season training camp to Abu Dhabi, in the United Arab Emirates, hoping the warm weather in the Arabian Gulf would prepare him for the 2010 Australian Open.

Once in Melbourne, it seemed the tactic might have worked. But then in the quarter-finals, up against Frenchman Jo-Wilfried Tsonga, his mysterious ailment struck yet again. "The invisible force attacked," he wrote. "I couldn't breathe." Requesting a toilet break, he ran to the locker-room and dropped to his knees in front of the toilet. "I felt as though I were vomiting up all of my strength," he later wrote.

Shortly afterwards, when Novak lost that match against Tsonga, he claims it was the nadir of his career. He says both his body and mind were broken. Clearly, some drastic change in his life was required.

It was his diet, it turns out, that was all wrong. His salvation came in the form of a Serbian alternative medicine practitioner and nutritionist called Dr Igor Četojević. Četojević had, by chance, been watching his countryman battling against Tsonga at the Aussie Open on TV. He was no tennis fan, but his wife Francesca was fond of the sport and, while they had been flipping through the channels at their home in Cyprus, she suggested they watch Novak play.

What happened next would change the course of Novak's life immeasurably. In an interview with United Arab Emirates newspaper *Gulf News*, Četojević later

OPPOSITE: Novak continued to suffer from breathing problems in the 2010 Australian Open.

explained how it was obvious to him it was Novak's digestive system that held the key to all his mysterious ailments – not asthma as the TV commentators kept saying. "From my observations and experience with Chinese traditional medicine, I could see that asthma was not the issue here," Četojević said. "Every time the commentator mentioned it, I said aloud: 'It's not asthma!' I know that generally most asthma symptoms appear in the morning – and Novak's match was in the afternoon. Also, if he really had an asthmatic condition, he would not have been able to play two excellent sets before the breathing difficulties appeared.

"I suspected that in Novak's case his problem breathing resulted from an imbalance in his digestive system, particularly from an accumulation of toxins in his large intestine. In traditional Chinese medicine, the lungs are paired with the large intestine."

Francesca urged her husband to offer Novak his expert help. So later that year, when Novak and the rest of the Serbian national team travelled to Split, in Croatia, for a July Davis Cup tie, through a mutual friend of Novak's father Srdjan, medic and player met up to discuss the problem. Četojević tested Novak for food allergies.

"I found that he was very sensitive to gluten, a protein present in wheat, one of the most common foods in Novak's diet," Četojević remembers. "He grew up, like so many young people, frequently eating wheat-based foods such as bread, pizza, pasta and pancakes."

Novak himself recalls that initial examination by Četojević being rather unorthodox, to say the least. He remembers how he was asked to place his left hand on his belly, and his right hand straight out to the side. The doctor pushed down on Novak's right arm as he resisted the pressure. Četojević then conducted the same experiment but this time with Novak grasping a slice of bread held against his stomach.

Initially Novak thought it was "madness". But bizarrely, he could feel that with the slice of bread on his stomach, he was noticeably weaker. "Like kryptonite," he said, in a nod to Superman.

More scientific tests followed, including a blood test called an enzyme-linked immunosorbent assay, which proved Novak was "strongly intolerant to wheat and dairy, and had a mild sensitivity to tomatoes". Četojević duly instructed his new client to stop eating bread and cheese, and to cut down on tomatoes.

"But doctor, my parents own a pizza parlour!" Novak replied.

Growing up, Novak had enjoyed a very traditional Balkan diet: plenty of meat, bread and dairy products. Italian cuisine was a strong influence too, so pasta was often on the menu. And thanks to his parents' restaurant, there were mountains of pizza constantly on offer. Novak believes it's possible his intolerance for bread and dairy products derives from a youth spent dining on the stuff.

Encouraged by Četojević, Novak agreed to try a gluten-free diet for two weeks. He completely cut out bread, pasta, cakes, wheat snacks, cereals and beer. At first he craved his old gluten-filled diet. But as the trial period progressed, he began to feel more energetic, lighter, "more explosive in my step". His mind felt clearer, too, and he slept far better.

After two weeks Četojević instructed his client to eat a bagel. The following day Novak felt sluggish, dizzy and congested – almost as if he had a hangover.

He quickly became a convert to this gluten-free diet, evangelical in his recommendation of it. His autobiography *Serve to Win* has as its subtitle "The 14-day gluten-free plan for physical and mental excellence" and is a blueprint for a gluten-free lifestyle.

ABOVE: Dr Igor Četojević has been widely credited with helping Novak reach the pinnacle of tennis.

The effects of the new diet were soon obvious to anyone who regularly watched him play. Although he lost a fair bit of weight (too much, some observers worried), his results improved drastically. The 2011 season was the most successful of his career: with Četojević accompanying him to many of his tournaments, he

played brilliantly, winning the Australian Open, Dubai, Indian Wells, Miami, Belgrade, Madrid, Rome, Wimbledon, Montreal and the US Open. Some say it's the greatest season ever executed by any male player in the history of the sport.

Emboldened by his success, Novak decided to invest in the gluten-free food industry. In 2015 he launched a range of snack foods called Djokolife. "Use your instinct and listen to your body before making decisions about your diet," he urged in the marketing blurb. "Choose to be healthy and happy. We all know what feeling bad means, but few know the real meaning of wellbeing. If you'd like to share my route I am sure you will benefit from it and discover the food that is right for each of you." Unfortunately the brand seems to have ceased trading since then.

Novak's autobiography goes into detail about his other healthy practices. He always tries to eat slowly, for example, in order to aid digestion. He drinks water close to room temperature, as iced water slows digestion. He avoids looking at screens of any kind while eating, and avoids "heavy conversations", so that he can concentrate on chewing. He tries to eat organic food.

Mindfulness is an important part of his daily routine. He says he spends 15 minutes a day meditating, and that it's as important to him as his physical training. He also tries to surround himself with open-minded people, so as to feel their positive energy, rather than closed-minded people who, he claims, radiate negativity.

Četojević later explained his influence in this area of mindfulness. "Novak needed to trust me," the medic said in the *Gulf News* interview. "Once he did, his progress was rapid. I taught him several breathing techniques that helped him sleep and focus on the present moment, the point at hand, rather than be caught up in a past shot that missed or a future shot that could seal the outcome of the match. The key is to stay in the present moment – something that is easier said than done."

Novak works hard to ensure he gets a good night's sleep every night. He tries to go to bed at the same time – between 11pm and midnight – and he wakes up at 7am every morning, even at weekends. He avoids caffeine, takes melatonin supplements, reads or does yoga just before bed, and stands with his face in sunlight soon after waking up.

Some of his ideas on health and diet are very eccentric, to say the least. Some would call them wacky. He claims that the power of thought and prayer can transform the molecules in water, for example. In an interview on the social media platform Instagram, in May 2020, he said the following: "I've seen people and I know some people that, through that energetical [sic] transformation, through the

OPPOSITE: Novak presenting his range of Djokolife products in Milan.

power of prayer, through the power of gratitude, they manage to turn the most toxic food or most polluted water, into the most healing water. Because water reacts and scientists have proven that molecules in the water react to our emotions, to what is being said."

In his autobiography, he claimed to have watched a test where a researcher directed loving energy towards one glass of water and cursed aggressively at a second glass. After a few days, the insulted glass "was tinted slightly green" while the loved one "was still bright and crystal clear". Clearly there is no scientific evidence for any of this.

In 2018, Novak appeared in a documentary series called *Transcendence: Live Life Beyond the Ordinary*, which analysed the way diet, stress and a change of mindset can help people live happier lives. Promoting the film, he explained his ideas on the power of the human mind and how we are all connected to the universe.

"We need to understand that we are connected on more levels than only on the physical," he said in an interview with the British magazine *Shortlist*. "We are connected with each other, with nature, with Earth, with the universe in an energetical [sic], higher vibrational sense. However you want to comprehend it, I feel like there is a higher order that created all this and all of us and we just have help that we are receiving."

Furthermore, Novak seemed to claim he believed in telekinesis – the power to move physical objects using one's mind. "You have this thing called telepathy, or this thing called telekinesis, or instinct, intuition. I feel like [these] are the gifts from this higher order, the source, the god, whatever, that allows us to understand the higher power and higher order in ourselves. We have the power to program our subconscious."

It's easy to dismiss these ideas as superstitious nonsense. But if they give Novak an extra edge on the tennis court, then why not allow him to indulge himself?

"Tennis is my love," he said in the same interview. "But I want to use it as a platform to make a positive difference. I know some people might say, 'He's a tennis player. What does he know about food or love or meditation or spirituality or science?' But I am attracted to all that. I like to encourage people to act, to look into liberating themselves more, to explore their superpowers."

In the time since his autobiography was published, Novak has adopted a plant-based diet: almost vegan, but with a little bit of fish thrown in. He says that after waking up he has a drink of water and lemon, followed by celery juice on

> I consider myself an open-minded and open-hearted person that respects and embraces [different] religions and knowledges that people have around the world that could enrich my life and my family's lives.

Novak Djokovic

YEAR-END RANKING

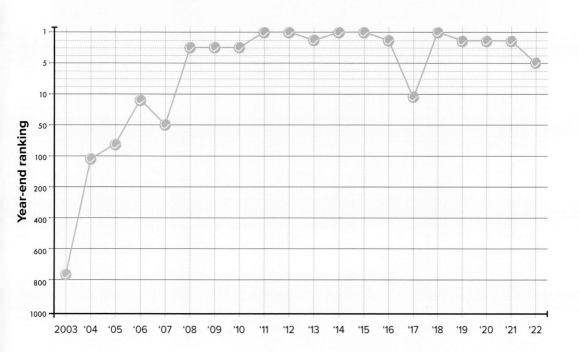

an empty stomach, plus a smoothie made of fruit, algae and supplements. It contributes to his "mental clarity", he claims. In general, he concentrates on fruit and salad during the first half of the day, in order to avoid expending energy on digestion. Quinoa, millet, rice, potatoes and sweet potatoes comprise much of the rest of his diet.

"It is a lifestyle more than just a diet," he explained recently. "Because you have ethical reasons as well, being conscious of what is happening in the animal world: the slaughtering of animals and farming. And there is obviously a huge impact with climate change. It's something that I'm really proud of. Hopefully that community grows even more and hopefully I can inspire other athletes [that] it is possible to be plant-based and to recover well and to have strength and to have muscles."

When it comes to religion, it's clear Novak believes in a Christian god. He wears a cross around his neck and on court regularly looks towards the heavens or makes the mark of the cross on his chest.

He's by no means devout, but he was brought up as a member of the Serbian Orthodox Church (part of Eastern Orthodox Christianity) and claims to be a believer. In April 2011, at an official ceremony in Belgrade, he was awarded the church's highest honour, the Order of St Sava. It was in recognition of his "active love" towards the church and his dedication to Serbian people, particularly those living in Kosovo. The presentation was made by His Holiness Serbian Patriarch Irenaeus.

"This award is certainly the most important I've ever been given," said Djokovic. "As an athlete and a religious person, it is hard for me to find appropriate words to describe my feelings of gratitude for the confidence I gain from the Holy Synod. I can only say that it can be earned only with hard work and self-belief, belief in your loved ones and in God."

In 2022, Novak suggested his beliefs aren't constrained by this one church. "I have been raised in an Orthodox Christian family, but I don't limit myself to that," he said in a press conference. "I consider myself an open-minded and open-hearted person that respects and embraces [different] religions and knowledges that people have around the world that could enrich my life and my family's lives."

In a world where religion often causes so much conflict, that's a very diplomatic answer.

THE MATCH

FRENCH OPEN

June 5th 2016

Roland Garros, Paris, France

Final: Novak Djokovic beat Andy Murray 3–6, 6–1, 6–2, 6–4

B y 2016, Novak was desperate to win the only Grand Slam title that still eluded him; almost too desperate. He had already won six Australian Opens, three Wimbledons and two US Opens. But Roland Garros remained beyond his grasp.

He had been close, mind: he'd reached the final in 2012, 2014 and 2015 and had four times been in the semi-final. But, like all great champions, he wanted to prove he had the ability to win Grand Slams on all surfaces, including clay.

In the lead-up to Paris, his clay record suggested something promising might be on the cards. He reached the finals of the Masters events in both Madrid and Rome, up against Andy Murray on both occasions, winning the first, losing the second. He arrived in Paris ranked number one in the world and full of confidence. The only question mark was his mental game, with possible distractions caused by media rumours that there were strains in his relationship with his wife Jelena (see Chapter 5, page 117).

If there were worries, he pushed them to the back of his mind. His progression through the draw at Roland Garros was sure and quick. It wasn't until the fourth round, against Roberto Bautista Agut, that he even lost a set. Then followed impressive wins over Tomáš Berdych and Dominic Thiem, until eventually he was in the final, up against Great Britain's Andy Murray again, their third meeting on clay in 2016.

Novak launched his attack early, breaking Murray's serve in the opening game, but the Scot delivered a sharp retort, breaking back twice and winning the first set. Novak's energy levels rose meteorically in the second set, which he wrapped up in just 36 minutes. He was equally dominant in the third.

It was emotions, though, rather than skills that won this match. Novak kept control of his while Murray allowed his temper to erupt. As the match began to ebb away from the Briton, he increasingly tried to place the blame on those around him. At one point Murray railed against a TV broadcaster whom he succeeded in having ejected from his team's spectator box for supposedly intruding in his eye line. Later he complained about the TV camera suspended above the court. His serving was atypically poor, too. By the end of the match the statistics showed only 50 per cent of his first serves had landed in, while he had won only 41 per cent of points on his second serve. The Parisian spectators had little sympathy for the British player, clearly siding with the Serbian instead, and making no effort to hide their partisanship.

By the fourth set, Novak was on a roll, breaking Murray twice for a 5–2 lead. After serving out the set and the match, he became only the eighth player in history to have captured all four Grand Slams, the others being Rod Laver, Rafael Nadal, Roger Federer, Andre Agassi, Roy Emerson, Don Budge and Fred Perry. Even more impressive was the fact that only two of those players – Budge in 1938 and Laver in 1962 and 1969 – had managed, like him, to hold all four of the major crowns at the same time.

OVERLEAF LEFT: Murray lost his temper while Novak kept his cool.

OVERLEAF RIGHT: Novak dominated Murray's serve in the final set, breaking him twice.

BELOW: Novak struggled as Murray broke his serve twice to take the first set.

"It's a thrilling moment," Novak said after the match. "One of the most beautiful I have had in my career. It's incredibly flattering to know that Rod Laver is the last one that managed to do that. There are not many words that can describe it. It's one of the ultimate challenges that you have as a tennis player. I'm very proud and very thrilled. I'm just so overwhelmed with having this trophy next to me that I'm just trying to enjoy this moment."

Clearly delighted, on victory he drew a heart shape in the clay on the court surface – a tribute, he said, to the Brazilian player Gustavo Kuerten who used to celebrate his Roland Garros wins in a similar fashion.

Novak described being in a sort of trance during the final point of the match. "I don't even remember what happened. It was really one of those things – moments where you just try to be there. It's like my spirit has left my body and I was observing my body."

Many others observing this body and its athletic exploits felt equally in a trance.

ABOVE: Novak draws a heart in the clay to celebrate his victory.

LEFT: Rod Laver was the last male player to hold all four Grand Slam titles at the same time.

OPPOSITE: Novak served out the fourth set and the match.

"
There are not many words that can describe it. It's one of the ultimate challenges that you have as a tennis player. I'm very proud and very thrilled. I'm just so overwhelmed with having this trophy next to me that I'm just trying to enjoy this moment.
"

Novak Djokovic

LEFT: Novak kisses his first French Open trophy.

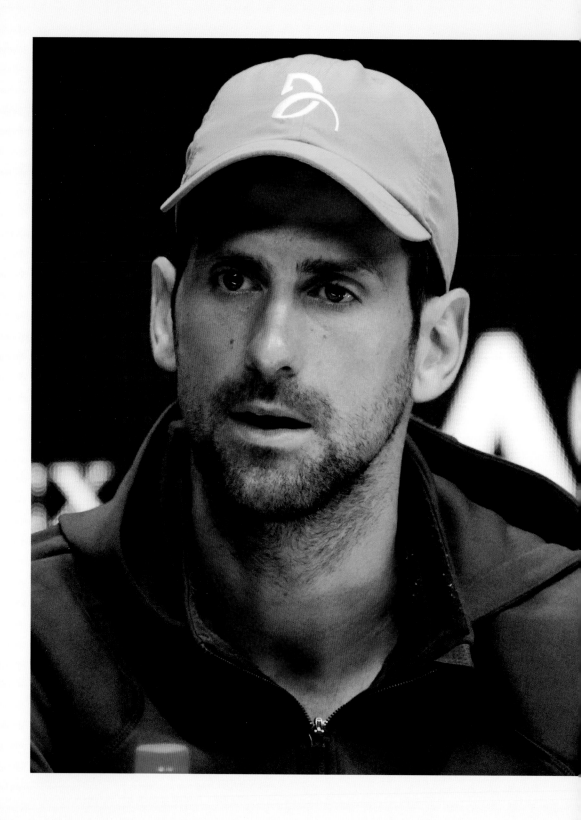

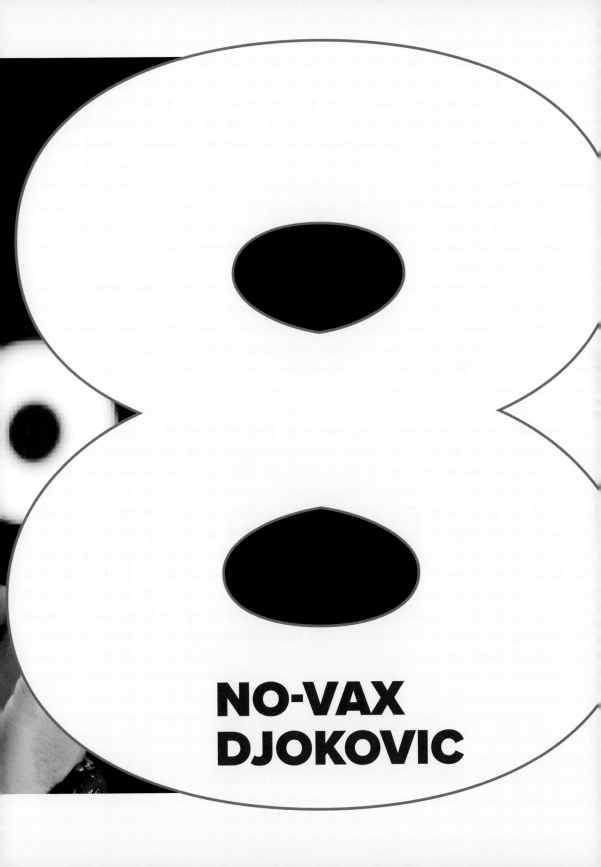

**NO-VAX
DJOKOVIC**

LEFT: Roland Garros was off-limits to the public during the Covid pandemic.

OVERLEAF: During the Covid pandemic, Novak organised an exhibition tour of tennis – the Adria Tour – at which social distancing was not enforced.

During the global Covid pandemic, Novak became embroiled in a vaccine debacle that almost derailed his career. While some might admire the player for standing up for his principles, in terms of public relations, it was a disaster.

Novak has always erred on the side of caution when it comes to traditional medicine (see Chapter 7). So, few were surprised when he expressed scepticism over the Covid vaccine. But given his status as a global superstar, he and his team might have handled the whole episode more diplomatically.

In 2020, just like the rest of the sporting world, the ATP tour shut down entirely for an extended period, as Covid raged around the planet. Novak initially made public his distrust of vaccinations. On its own, this wouldn't have caused much controversy. However, in June of that year he organised and embarked on an exhibition tour of Croatia and Serbia – called the Adria Tour – with fans permitted to attend matches, despite the strict social-distancing measures in place in many other parts of the world. In addition to Novak, other players due to compete included Dominic Thiem, Alexander Zverev and Grigor Dimitrov. During the Croatian leg, the latter tested positive for Covid, after which the controversial tour was abandoned. Social media posts showed players hugging, shaking hands and dancing together during the event. Several other players, including Novak, later tested positive.

Crucially, though, Novak and his colleagues were not breaking the law in the countries they were competing in. Novak himself insisted the tournament had been sanctioned by the government. "You can also criticise us and say this is maybe dangerous but it's not up to me to make the calls about what is right or wrong for health," he added. "We are doing what the Serbian government is telling us and hopefully we soon will get back on tour collectively. Of course, lives have been lost and that's horrible to see, in

the region and worldwide. But life goes on, and we as athletes are looking forward to competing."

Inevitably, since he was the world number-one-ranked player at the time, there was a backlash against him in the international media. Public opinion worsened when the player voiced his opposition to the Covid vaccine. In August 2020, he explained himself to *The New York Times*. "My issue here with vaccines is if someone is forcing me to put something in my body," he said. "That I don't want. For me that's unacceptable. I am not against vaccination of any kind, because who am I to speak about vaccines when there are people that have been in the field of medicine and saving lives around the world? I'm sure that there are vaccines that have little side effects that have helped people and helped stop the spread of some infections around the world."

It was around this time that Novak invested in a Danish biotech firm that claimed to be developing a non-vaccine treatment for Covid (see page 139).

Things came to a head towards the end of 2021 when Novak registered to play in the 2022 Australian Open, the following January. The Australian government, which had imposed some of the strictest Covid rules of all Western nations, stated that anyone who wished to enter the country would have to show proof of vaccination, or proof of an "acute major medical condition" that would exempt them.

By this time, Novak's anti-vaccination status was a global discussion point. His father Srdjan didn't help matters by appearing on Serbian TV and claiming his son was being "blackmailed" into being vaccinated. Everyone assumed Novak wouldn't be allowed to compete in Melbourne.

Then, suddenly, on January 4th 2022, the player posted a picture of himself with bundles of luggage at an airport, alongside the message, "Today I'm heading Down Under with an exemption permission. Let's go 2022!!"

On arrival in Australia, all hell broke loose. Immigration officials questioned Novak's paperwork, revoked his visa and denied him entry. Pending a final decision from the authorities, he was forced to remain in a detention hotel. His father claimed he was being "held captive". Multiple lawyers became involved and after much toing and froing he was granted permission to enter Australia. He was going to compete in the Open after all.

Or was he? The majority of Australians, living through ultra-strict Covid restrictions and watching infection numbers continue to soar, perhaps justifiably felt it was unfair to allow Novak entry simply because he was a famous tennis player. Finally, after spending 11 days cloistered in his hotel, on January 16th Novak was deported from Australia and flew back home to Serbia. Australia's immigration minister claimed the player's presence in Australia risked "civil unrest" because he was a "talisman of anti-vaccination sentiment". The game was up.

Novak realised he needed to make his side of the story public. In February of that year he invited BBC journalist Amol Rajan to visit him at his tennis centre in Belgrade. In an interview that was broadcast all over the world, he conceded that, when crossing national frontiers, he should be subject to exactly the same Covid restrictions as anyone else. And he accepted that his refusal to be vaccinated would force him to miss many tournaments. "That is the price that I'm willing to pay. Because the principles of decision-making of my body are more important than any title and anything else."

Novak tried to distance himself from the anti-vaxxers, as the Covid vaccination opposers became known. "I was never against vaccination," he told the BBC.

PREVIOUS, LEFT: Novak and Alexander Zverev before their Adria Tour match.

PREVIOUS, RIGHT: Novak arriving in Australia in January 2022.

LEFT: Novak lost the legal battle to compete in the Australian Open and was deported.

PLAYERS TO REACH FINALS AT ALL FOUR GRAND SLAM

- Australia
- French
- Wimbledon
- US

Novak Djokovic

9
7
Grand slam finals
36
10
10

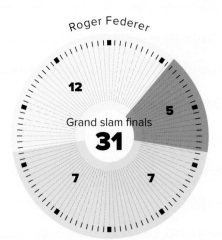

Roger Federer

12
5
Grand slam finals
31
7
7

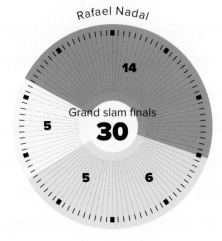

Rafael Nadal

14
5
Grand slam finals
30
5
6

Ivan Lendl

2
5
Grand slam finals
19
8
4

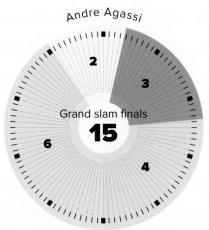

Andre Agassi

2
3
Grand slam finals
15
6
4

"I understand and support fully the freedom to choose whether you want to get vaccinated or not. I understand that globally, everyone is trying to put a big effort to handling this virus and seeing, hopefully, an end to this virus. And vaccination is probably the biggest effort that was made – probably half of the planet was vaccinated and I fully respect that. But I've always represented and always supported the freedom to choose what you put in your body. For me, that is essential. It is really the principle of understanding what is right and what is wrong for you.

"And me as an elite professional athlete, I have always carefully reviewed, assessed everything that comes in from the supplements, food, the water that I drink or sports drinks – anything that comes into my body as a fuel. Based on the information that I got, I decided not to take the vaccine. I am part of a very global sport that is played every single week in a different location, so I understand the consequences of my decision."

The interview silenced some of his critics, but not all. By now, many were calling him "No-vax Djokovic". As the 2022 season progressed, his woes went from bad to worse. He withdrew from the Indian Wells and Miami Masters tournaments since his status as an unvaccinated foreigner meant he was refused

ABOVE: Carlos Alcaraz triumphed in the 2022 US Open in Novak's absence.

entry to the United States. He reached the quarter-finals at Roland Garros and beat Nick Kyrgios to secure his seventh Wimbledon title but by June he had lost his world number-one ranking. Later that summer, he was still barred from entry into the United States so that he couldn't play in the US Open.

By January 2023, Novak had embarked on a charm offensive. Despite the previous year's visa debacle, he was granted access to the Australian Open. "I'm very grateful for the kind of energy and reception, love and support," he said after his first-round match. "The amount of positive experiences I had in Australia overwhelm the negative experience of last year."

A fortnight later he was celebrating his tenth Aussie Open victory – a record no other man has ever come close to. It looked like all was forgiven. The prodigal son had returned.

> And me as an elite professional athlete, I have always carefully reviewed, assessed everything that comes in from the supplements, food, the water that I drink or sports drinks – anything that comes into my body as a fuel. Based on the information that I got, I decided not to take the vaccine.

Novak Djokovic

THE MATCH

FRENCH OPEN

June 11th 2021

Roland Garros, Paris, France

Semi-final: Novak Djokovic beat Rafael Nadal 3–6, 6–3, 7–6, 6–2

Since 2017, Rafa Nadal had reigned supreme as men's champion at Roland Garros. It took a certain Serb, playing one of the greatest clay-court matches of his career, to end his 35-match winning streak and knock him from his perch.

"It was one of these matches you can remember forever," said Novak after beating the Spaniard in a four-set semi-final. So gripping, in fact, that the French authorities decided to waive their strict Covid restrictions in force at the time, permitting fans to stay out beyond the 11 pm curfew.

Although Novak had been playing clinical, highly effective tennis throughout the tournament, when it came to his semi-final clash against Nadal, he started nervously, unable to find his rhythm. It wasn't long before the defending champion had raced to a 5–0 lead. Novak avoided the bagel, but still failed to fight back in that first set.

The second set saw some ferocious tennis, as both players were forced to defend break points. Even at set point, Novak delivered an uncharacteristic double fault, and was forced again into a defensive position before finally equalising at one set all.

It was the third set, however, that provided the most thrilling action of all. Former professionals and experienced pundits alike often cite it as the most exciting set of tennis ever witnessed at Roland Garros. Despite the depleted crowd – due to pandemic restrictions there were only 5,000 fans on Court Philippe Chatrier – the atmosphere was as tense and as electric as anything you'd experience at a fully attended final. At 3–6, 6–3, 3–3, after more than two and a half hours on court, with both men having won 84 points, they had reached total parity. Fans of both players ramped up the noise and the partisanship. At times it felt like a Davis Cup tie rather than an under-spectated semi-final.

With an icily clinical dropshot, Novak saved set point and forced the tiebreak. Nadal started it badly, with a double fault, and then later sent an easy volley

OPPOSITE: Novak celebrates winning a tense third set.

OVERLEAF: The atmosphere was electric despite the depleted crowd.

OPPOSITE: Nadal took the second set to equalise.

ABOVE: Nadal received treatment on his ankle early in the fourth set.

RIGHT: After defeating Nadal, Novak went on to win the final against Tsitsipas.

OVERLEAF: Novak named the battle his top match at Roland Garros.

long. After a set lasting 93 minutes, it was Novak who secured the tiebreak.

By now it was 10.40pm, with just 20 minutes to go until the official curfew. Sure enough, over the stadium tannoy an announcement started. At first it was greeted by boos and catcalls – that was until the fans realised they were being given permission to stay until the end. Jeers promptly turned to cheers.

Early in the fourth set, Nadal started limping and asked for treatment on his ankle. It looked like the game was up. Then Novak broke his opponent for a 4–2 lead, eventually closing the set and the match 6–2.

"Definitely the best match that I was part of ever in Roland Garros for me," Novak said afterwards. "And top-three matches that I ever played in my entire career, considering quality of tennis, playing my biggest rival on the court where he has been the dominant force in the last 15-plus years, and the atmosphere which was completely electric."

The Serb was gracious in his victory. "It's hard to find words bigger than all the superlatives you can think of for Rafa's achievements in Roland Garros. I mean, he has been the most dominant player of the Roland Garros history. The amount of wins that he has made on this court is incredible. Each time you step on the court with him, you know that you have to climb Mount Everest to win against this guy here."

Everest successfully summited, Novak then faced Greek player Stefanos Tsitsipas in the final, beating him in five sets to secure his second French Open title.

MAKING
HISTORY

Novak's coach Goran Ivanišević is perhaps more than a little biased when it comes to appraising his charge: "I will remember him as the greatest player of all time and a man who broke all the limits. It's like he came straight from that show *The Twilight Zone*: unreal results, unreal shots, unreal everything ..." His praise may be effusive but it's not an exaggeration. Once Novak has retired from tennis, many will look back on him as the greatest player of all time.

"Sometimes I watch him and I don't think it's possible what he is doing – while I'm watching him do it," Ivanišević continues in an interview with the website Tennis Majors. "And he not only does it again, but does it even better. He will be remembered as a great fighter who proved that anything is possible."

Novak will be remembered for many things: for his at times turbulent childhood, growing up under the shadow of the Yugoslav Wars and the NATO bombing of his home city Belgrade; for his very eccentric espousal of unorthodox medical practices; for his principled (some would say stubborn) refusal to receive the Covid vaccine and the subsequent damage to his international image; but mostly for his tennis – arguably the greatest tennis played by any human being ever.

How are we to measure his achievements on the court? The length of time ranked at number one in the world and the number of ATP tournament titles are two important metrics. As this book was being prepared, this was over 390 weeks (more than any other player, male or female) and 96 singles titles. But far more important than that, as we analyse in depth in the next chapter, is his total tally of Grand Slam singles titles (currently 24).

Amid all this incredible achievement there are two seasons of his career when Novak shone at his very brightest: 2011 and 2015.

In 2011, he triumphed in ten tournaments, including three

OPPOSITE: Novak and Nadal are fierce rivals who respect each other enormously.

OVERLEAF: Novak finishes an incredible 2015 season, winning the US Open.

Grand Slams (the Australian Open, Wimbledon and the US Open) and five ATP Masters events. Four years later he topped that by winning 11 tournaments, including the same three Grand Slams, plus six ATP Masters events and the ATP Finals. Given the calibre of opponents he was up against in both years – such as Roger Federer, Rafa Nadal and Andy Murray – these two seasons might be considered the best performances of the 21st century. And in men's tennis, they are among the greatest single-season records of the professional era.

NUMBER OF WEEKS SPENT AS WORLD NUMBER ONE

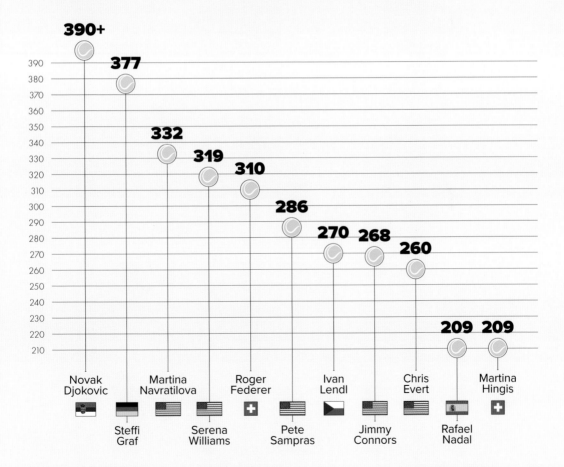

	Weeks
Novak Djokovic	390+
Steffi Graf	377
Martina Navratilova	332
Serena Williams	319
Roger Federer	310
Pete Sampras	286
Ivan Lendl	270
Jimmy Connors	268
Chris Evert	260
Rafael Nadal	209
Martina Hingis	209

There's another key area where Novak will be remembered, and that's thanks to his involvement as co-founder of the Professional Tennis Players Association. He established the association in 2021, in the midst of the Covid pandemic, along with Canadian player Vasek Pospisil. Their purpose was to "create transparency and fairness throughout decision-making in professional tennis". It is open to both male and female professional players.

Two years on, the association's mission statement is as follows: "By maximising player voices, advocating for player health and wellbeing, and creating on and off-court opportunities for players, the PTPA is working to build an equitable, modernised and sustainable competitive tennis environment for today's players and generations of players to come."

Many within the sport view the PTPA as a challenge to the existing players' unions – the ATP and the WTA. If Novak's association gains traction, it could foment a major schism in world tennis. Indeed, the PTPA claims that the ATP has "grown into an anti-competitive organisation that it once vowed to protect the players from".

The PTPA certainly has some very noble aims. It campaigns for equitable prize money, off-court earning opportunities, retirement pensions, and travel and accommodation standards.

"Tennis players have the right to share fairly in the economic activity and wealth of tennis, which players have helped generate, underpinned by fair and just pay and working conditions," it states on its website. It wants to protect players' rights, including commercial control of their names, images and likenesses. It wants to beef up player welfare and security on the tour. The association now has eight active players on its executive committee, including the two co-founders, Novak and Pospisil, and players from the United States, Spain, Poland, China and Tunisia.

Novak deserves to be congratulated for establishing the PTPA. From the outside, it seems to be a mostly altruistic effort. Given his own fame, fortune and power, it's not an organisation that will particularly benefit him personally, however it could transform the lives of lower-ranked tennis players who regularly struggle for money, representation and to get their voices heard. If the PTPA succeeds, future tennis players and fans might look back on it as Novak's greatest gift to the sport.

OPPOSITE: With the Wimbledon trophy in 2011.

ABOVE: Novak co-founded the Professional Tennis Players Association with Canadian Vasek Pospisil in 2021.

Tennis players have the right to share fairly in the economic activity and wealth of tennis, which players have helped generate, underpinned by fair and just pay and working conditions.

PTPA website

GOLDEN YEARS: 2011 AND 2015

2011

Won 41
consecutive matches
from the start of the
year until June 3rd
(French Open semi-final)

Won a then-record
5 masters
titles in the season:
Indian Wells, Miami, Canada,
Madrid and Rome

Won 10
titles on three
different surfaces

Beat Nadal and Federer
10 times
losing only once
(to Federer in
the French Open)

2015

Reached the final of
**every
Grand Slam**
winning three of them

Won a record
**31
matches**
over other Top-10 players

Beat his own
Masters record in
**winning
six titles**
Indian Wells, Miami,
Monte Carlo, Rome,
Shanghai, Paris, plus the
ATP World Tour Finals

Set an all-time ATP
rankings points record of
16,950

THE MATCH

WIMBLEDON

July 10th 2022

All England Club, London, UK

Final: Novak Djokovic beat Nick Kyrgios 4–6, 6–3, 6–4, 7–6

After losing to an indomitable Novak in the 2022 Wimbledon final, Nick Kyrgios admitted: "He is a bit of a god." And it's true that the Serbian did display some divine tennis to secure his seventh Wimbledon title and the 21st Grand Slam title of his career.

On paper, the Australian should have been better prepared for the encounter since he had avoided having to play his semi-final match when Rafa Nadal dropped out with an injury. And Novak certainly looked more tired as, during the first set of the final, he struggled to read Kyrgios's mighty serve and even found himself out-rallied on occasions. Serving to stay in that first set, Novak then double-faulted on break point.

The way both players wore their baseball hats during the match was perhaps representative of how they approach their tennis. Kyrgios, the less conventional player, had his turned backwards, while Novak, who is far more orthodox, wore his the right way round.

In the second set the Serb gradually found his footing. On one of Kyrgios's service games he stunned his opponent by playing four faultless returns of first serve, and breaking to love.

As the third set progressed, the Australian player's notoriously short temper began to fray, to the delight of many fans present. Much of his anger was directed against his team in their box, courtside. There was further ire when a female fan called out just as the Australian was serving. Kyrgios let loose a swear word, perhaps understandably, but it resulted in a code violation for an audible obscenity. The Australian demanded the umpire eject the offending fan. "She's distracting me when I'm serving in Wimbledon final. There's no other bigger occasion," he said. "It nearly cost me the game. Why's she still here? She's drunk out of her mind, so kick her out," he complained. "I know exactly who it is – she's the one who looks like she's had about 700 drinks."

The spectators, including Prince William, and actors Kate Winslet, Tom Cruise, Tom Hiddleston and Jason Statham, seemed bemused. There was further interruption when a protestor was led away by security after bringing to attention the case of the Chinese player Peng Shuai.

While Kyrgios fumed, though, Novak very much kept his cool. During that third set the Serb blasted 14 winners and committed only two unforced errors. The momentum was still very much with him.

Kyrgios served strongly again in the fourth set, battling hard to keep his nose ahead. Eventually a tiebreak was required. This went Novak's way, handing him the championship.

On victory, he sympathised with his opponent, placing an arm around his shoulders. Then he spread his arms to embrace the crowd, brought his right hand to his heart, and crouched down to touch the hallowed turf of Wimbledon's Centre Court. As is now his habit, he plucked a few blades of grass and ate them, smiling all the while.

BELOW: Novak upped his game in the second set with masterful returns of serve.

She's distracting me when I'm serving in Wimbledon final. There's no other bigger occasion. It nearly cost me the game.

Nick Kyrgios

LEFT: Novak won the fourth-set tiebreak to take the match.

In the past, relations between these two players had been more than a little frosty. Nonetheless, once the match was over, both lavished each other with praise. "I never thought I would say many nice things about you, considering the relationship," said Novak. "Okay, officially it is a bromance."

On receiving his trophy, Novak was understandably a little emotional. He explained how Wimbledon had motivated him to excel in tennis ever since he had first watched Pete Sampras win the tournament on TV when he was a little kid in the mountain resort of Kopaonik. It was back then that he first asked his parents to buy him a tennis racket.

"My first image of tennis was grass and Wimbledon. I always dreamed of coming here," he said. "Realising a childhood dream and winning this trophy, every single time it gets more meaningful and special. I'm really blessed and thankful to be standing here with the trophy. It is the most special tennis court in the world."

ABOVE LEFT: The emotion of winning match point.

ABOVE: The two players have clashed in the past but are now good friends.

LEFT: Novak loves to celebrate winning Wimbledon by nibbling Centre Court grass.

OPPOSITE: An emotional Novak is interviewed after receiving his trophy.

10

WHAT
THE
FUTURE
HOLDS

LEFT: Nadal, Novak and Federer at the 2022 Laver Cup.

When this book was published, Novak was 36 years old. In the old days, reaching one's mid-thirties was a sign of superannuation in professional tennis. It would generally signal retirement from the singles game as the physical rigours took their toll. If you stayed fit, you might expect a few more years playing doubles.

But by the turn of the millennium, that had all changed. Players began to take their fitness regimes more seriously than ever before. By incorporating comprehensive stretching routines, targeted gym workouts, yoga, ice baths, daily physiotherapy and the like, they were able to stave off the physical deterioration normally associated with middle age.

All three of the champions who have dominated 21st-century men's tennis have triumphed in Grand Slams after their 35th birthdays. Roger Federer, for example, was 35 when he won the 2017 Australian Open and the 2017 Wimbledon title; he was 36 when he took the 2018 Australian Open. Rafa Nadal was 35 when, in 2022, he won the Australian Open, and he added that year's French Open two days after turning 36. And Novak was 36 when he won both the French and US Open in 2023. (There's a Grand Slam winner even older than these three, and that's Ken Rosewall, who won the 1972 Australian Open at 37; however, he enjoyed a fairly easy route to victory as many of the world's top players had backed out due to a dispute between the International Tennis Federation and the nascent professional circuits.)

Given Novak's current supreme levels of fitness, and his astoundingly disciplined attitude to health (see Chapter 7), there's no reason to suggest he can't continue competing at the very top level for several years yet. He shows no signs of slowing down. Only a fool would bet against him notching up at least a couple more Grand Slam titles.

"I am motivated to win as many Slams as possible," he said after winning his 22nd at the 2023 Australian Open.

"At this stage of my career, these trophies are the biggest motivational factor of why I still compete. That's the case without a doubt. I never really liked comparing myself to others, but of course it's a privilege to be part of the discussion as one of the greatest players of all time. If people see me this way, of course it's very flattering because I know that I give as much effort and energy into trying to win Slams as anybody else.

"I still have lots of motivation. Let's see how far it takes me. I really don't want to stop here. I don't have intention to stop here. I feel great about my tennis. I know that when I'm feeling good physically, mentally present, I have a chance to win any Slam against anybody."

In the United States, sports journalists love to describe the very greatest sportsmen and women by using the term GOAT, meaning "greatest of all time". When it comes to tennis, whatever nation you're from, the GOAT is determined by the number of Grand Slam singles titles a player has won. It is the yardstick by which all champions are measured. While the total number of weeks ranked at number one in the world is also important, as is the total tally of ATP or WTA tournament titles, without question, when it comes to a player's historical legacy,

OPPOSITE:
Serena Williams
has dominated the
women's game in
the 21st century with
23 Grand Slam
singles' titles.

ABOVE: Nadal sits
just behind Novak
with 22 Grand Slam
singles titles.

ABOVE RIGHT: For
decades Margaret
Court held the grand
slam singles record
with 24 in total.

Grand Slam singles titles are the most important metric of all. The goal of all leading players is to notch up as many as possible.

So where does Novak rank among the GOATs of tennis? Sports fans are privileged to have witnessed this early 21st-century era in which three men (Novak, Federer and Nadal) and one woman (Serena Williams) have been battling for the Grand Slam singles record. To witness one true great at the height of his/her powers is brilliant enough, but to witness four is just greedy.

Historically, Australian player Margaret Court was top of the tree, with 24 Grand Slam singles titles. However, 11 of those were Australian Open victories, and the lion's share of her playing career took place during the 1960s when tennis was still an amateur sport, and when fewer international players made the long journey to Melbourne to contest the Australian Open. Hence her domination Down Under.

But with his 2023 US Open win, Novak has equalled her record and joins her in the top spot. Second and third place go to Serena Williams and Rafael Nadal with 23 and 22 titles respectively. No other active player, male or female, is even close to this number. By the time you read this, Novak may already have won

further Grand Slams. Granted, he's 36 years old now, with younger players snapping at his heels, but given his incredible fitness and mental fortitude, he could end up eclipsing Court. Why not 25 Grand Slam titles? Or even more? It's not unthinkable. And the prospect of further clashes between Novak and Nadal is something all tennis fans would relish.

"I don't know how many more years I'm going to play or how many more Slams I'm going to play," Novak said after his 22nd. "It depends on various things. It doesn't depend only on my body. I think it's extremely important for me, first to have the support and love from the close ones, and [the] ability to play and keep the balance with the private life. But, at the same time, have the mental clarity or aspirations to really strive to chase these trophies. Physically I can keep myself fit. I still feel there is time ahead of me. Let's see how far I go."

Novak's coach, Goran Ivanišević, is equally optimistic. "I am sure that he can go on for a few more years – two, three, four, I can't put an exact number on it," he said in an interview with the website Tennis Majors. "His body is in perfect shape because he takes care of it so meticulously; he is always introducing something fresh into his regime. For how long can he keep going like this, it depends on his motivations, desire, goals ... A few more years for sure."

OPPOSITE: Novak congratulates Nadal on his victory in their 2022 quarter-final at Roland Garros.

RIGHT: Novak's coach believes his career will continue for at least a few more years.

ABOVE: Nadal has been a worthy opponent throughout Novak's career.

However superhuman the athlete, eventually both body and mind are forced to accept the passing of time. One day, Novak will have to concede – hopefully at a time of his choosing but possibly involuntarily through physical wear and tear – that enough is enough.

How will he fill his time once he exits the professional game? Given his godlike popularity at home in Serbia, some have suggested he ought to carve a role for himself in politics. Just look at George Weah, the Liberian footballer who became president of his nation. Or Manny Pacquiao, the Filipino world champion boxer who became a senator. Given the complicated machinations of Serbian politics, though, Novak might be wise to steer clear of public office.

Saša Ozmo, the tennis journalist with Balkan TV channel and website Sport Klub, has followed his countryman's career especially closely. He points to Novak's founding of and current involvement in the Professional Tennis Players

NOVAK – BOOK OF RECORDS

Record
390+
weeks as top
of ATP rankings

Year-end
NO. 1
a record seven times

24
Slams won, more than any
other male player

Only player to
have held all
4
major titles on
3
different surfaces at the
same time (Wimbledon 2015
through to French 2016)

Only player to win all
four Grand Slams,
all
9 Masters
tournaments and the
ATP Tour finals
more than once

Most wins
over Top-10 ranked
players of any player
in Open era (251)

One of only
two players to have
beaten Rafael Nadal at
the French Open, and
the only one
to do it twice

Djokovic has had
10
20-match winning
streaks in his career

Association, and suggests, after his career is over, he may ramp up his involvement in sports administration. But politics itself? No way. "Novak is an athlete, not a politician," Ozmo insists, totally scotching the idea. "He has said numerous times that he doesn't have any ambitions in getting involved with any kind of politics."

Could he end up coaching other professional players on the tour? The prospect of continuing that relentless grind of global travel on the ATP tour must be off-putting for him. However, he has, in the recent past, said he would love to share his skills with younger players. "I try to pass on to new generations everything that I've learned. Knowledge can be a curse if you don't use it. What am I supposed to do when I retire? Take it to my grave so that those who come after me are unable to benefit from my philosophy, work methods and approach? For me, it's only logical that the next step should be to pass my knowledge on to others. I see myself in various roles in the future and I am glad that I can also develop as a coach."

For now, though, retirement is far from his mind. He insists he is still as motivated as ever about competing. "For me it's about, first of all, having good emotions and positive feelings on the court [and] practice court," he said at the end of 2022. "One thing is to win big trophies, and it's a fairy tale. But you've got to go through hardship, a lot of hardship, a lot of difficult days and challenging tasks in order to push yourself, motivate yourself, to get to this level and [have] a chance to win. That's, for me, the most important thing."

And when that motivation finally does ebb, Novak claims he will remain in the sport. "I will always stay in tennis in whatever shape, form or role," he said. "I feel like the love for the tennis will never fade away."

ABOVE: Novak says he would love to share his skills with a new generation of players.

"I still have lots of motivation. Let's see how far it takes me. I really don't want to stop here. I don't have intention to stop here.

Novak Djokovic

THE MATCH

AUSTRALIAN OPEN

January 29th 2023

Melbourne Park, Melbourne, Australia

Final: Novak Djokovic beat Stefanos Tsitsipas 6–3, 7–6, 7–6

Ten Australian Open titles. To triumph ten times in singles at the same Grand Slam is a phenomenal achievement in tennis. In fact, only one other man (Rafa Nadal with his 14 French Opens) and one woman (Margaret Court with her 11 Australian Opens) has managed to pull off such a feat.

Novak himself, who played the final while nursing a tear in his hamstring – an injury sustained earlier that January at a tournament in Adelaide – called it "the biggest victory in my life". If that's an exaggeration, it's not a wild one.

Remember, the previous year the Serbian player had been barred from competing in this tournament because he wasn't vaccinated against Covid (see Chapter 8). To come back a year later, to shake off the criticism from the many Australians still upset at his actions, and to compete at a stellar level, even with a hamstring tear, is all testament to what an incredible champion Novak really is.

Tsitsipas must have been especially disappointed, knowing his opponent wasn't in perfect physical condition. The tournament director Craig Tiley explained afterwards: "This guy, he had a three-centimetre tear in his hammy. It's hard to believe that someone can do what they do with those types of injuries."

There was further distraction in the form of Novak's father Srdjan, who had been spotted earlier in the tournament alongside a group of pro-Vladimir Putin supporters – all waving Russian flags and chanting messages of support for the Russian leader and his invasion of Ukraine. He wasn't in the stadium for his son's match.

Novak started strongly, dominating his Greek opponent during the first set. In the second set, Tsitsipas began to establish a rhythm, matching Novak point for point and game for game. At 5–4 the Greek even managed to reach set point. This was arguably the key point of the entire match. Instead of defending, Novak – in his blue shorts and red, white and blue check shirt – became more aggressive than ever. He punished Tsitsipas's hesitation with a vicious forehand to bring the set level at five-all. There followed a tense tiebreak in which Novak came out on top, helped by some wayward forehands from the Greek.

The third set unfolded in much the same way, with little separating the two players. Again a tiebreak was needed.

By now Novak had switched to an all-blue check shirt. With the Serb 5–3 up in the tiebreak, there ensued an extraordinary rally of 27 shots, with both players zigzagging up and down and back and forth across the court. Novak eventually lost the point and looked utterly exhausted. But he regrouped, taking the tiebreak 7–5 – and with it the match – with a forehand that landed slap-bang on the sideline. After pointing to his head and his heart, he thanked his opponent, the umpire and the crowd, and then he looked skywards before delivering a few words to his god. Grand Slam number 22. He was now tied with Rafa Nadal on the all-time record. And he had also regained the number-one spot in the world rankings.

BELOW: Novak won the match with a forehand landing right on the line.

After grasping the magnitude of his victory, Novak finally allowed all his emotions to come to the fore. He wept as he clambered up into the players' box to celebrate with his mother and support team. The tears continued at the side of the

LEFT: Speaking to his god after victory.

BELOW : A new jacket celebrates his 22nd Grand Slam singles title.

court, where he treated himself to a private moment by covering his head with a towel, his torso convulsing.

Later he put on a jacket, newly emblazoned with the number 22, before accepting the Norman Brookes Challenge Cup, the weight and feel of which was by now very familiar to him. "This is one of the most challenging tournaments that I have ever played in my life," he said, in reference to his hamstring injury and his banishment from the same event the previous year. "Not playing last year, coming back this year. I want to thank all the people who made me feel welcome. There is a reason why I have played my best tennis on this court. It is a long journey. All my team and family knows what we have been through in the past four or five weeks and this is probably the biggest victory of my life."

Novak's coach Goran Ivanišević was effusive with his praise. "The guy is unbelievable. I don't know how to describe in words. I thought I saw everything, and then you see this."

Afterwards, Novak explained the significance his astounding sporting success could have on a nation as small as Serbia. "I truly believe and I hope that, especially young people in Serbia, find a lot of inspiration in what I do, what I have achieved, so it motivates them to grab a racket or whatever they do, whether it's sport or any other area of life. Dream big and nurture those dreams.

"Coming from countries like Serbia with almost zero tennis tradition, it makes [it a] far bigger challenge to reach the big heights and great heights. You have to pave your own way and become the first in something. For me, appreciation for everything that I have achieved in life is greater because of knowing how I started."

"Coming from countries like Serbia with almost zero tennis tradition, it makes [it a] far bigger challenge to reach the big heights and great heights. You have to pave your own way and become the first in something. For me, appreciation for everything that I have achieved in life is greater because of knowing how I started."

Novak Djokovic

LEFT: A full crowd witnessed Novak claiming his 10th Australian Open.

CONCLUSION

On September 10th 2023, Novak Djokovic defeated Daniil Medvedev in the final of the US Open, 6–3, 7–6, 6–3.

Yes, he won his third Grand Slam of the year. Yes, he regained his number one spot in the world rankings. Yes, he extended his all-time record at the top of the world rankings to a staggering 390 weeks. But there's only one number that matters in all of this: 24. Novak has now amassed 24 Grand Slam singles titles, more than any other male player and equal to the female record (set by Margaret Court back in the early 1970s).

No one should underestimate the importance of this. The Serbian is now the greatest male tennis player ever to have wielded a racket ... by a country mile. "To make history of this sport is something truly remarkable and special," he said after receiving his trophy. "When I was seven, eight, I wanted to become the best player in the world and win the Wimbledon trophy. But then I started to dream new dreams and set new objectives, new goals. I never imagined I would be here standing with you talking about 24 Slams."

In the run-up to the final, Novak said his family and support team knew it was a bad idea to mention – even hint at – the historical significance of a potential 24th title. The player himself did his utmost not to let the gravity of the situation prey on his mind.

Once his match against Russian player Daniil Medvedev had started, as a psychological tactic, this initially seemed to work. Dominating the first set, Novak ensured he took the ball early, shortening the rallies wherever possible. After all, his opponent was nine years his junior and understandably often faster around the court. But Novak was soon 6–3 up.

In the second set, however, the Serb started to struggle. In an attempt to throw the Russian off his stride, he made the unusual decision to employ serve-and-volley tactics. It worked but he was clearly in some discomfort. At 3–3 he fell to the ground in exhaustion. "I felt like I was losing air on so many occasions," he explained later. "And my legs as well. I don't recall being so exhausted after rallies as I have been in the second set."

The entire match ended up hinging on the tiebreak at the end of this second

OPPOSITE: Novak lifts the trophy in a jacket emblazoned with "24" to mark the occasion.

set. At first, Medvedev edged ahead, taking the lead 5–4 with a brilliant dropshot to conclude an amazing 23-shot rally. But then Novak fought back, blasting his opponent with indomitable serving. In all, the second set lasted for 104 minutes, depleting the energy reserves of both men.

By the third set, Novak had the measure of his opponent, breaking his serve twice. A true fighter, though, Medvedev raged on. Finally, at championship point, the Russian netted a forehand to grant Novak the fourth US Open title of his career.

How did the greatest of all time feel the moment he had won? "Relief mostly," he admitted. "That's why I didn't celebrate maybe as I did in Roland Garros. I didn't fall to the floor or jump out of joy. I was so relieved when I saw his forehand in the net. Out of respect I wanted to go quicker to the net to shake hands and exchange words."

Immediately after that handshake, Novak headed straight for his six-year-old daughter Tara to give her a hug. Unusually she was sitting in the front row, not in the players' box. It turns out Tara had been a source of extra fuel for her father during the match. "She was facing me when I was sitting on the bench," Novak recalled. "And she smiled at me. Every single time I needed that innocent child energy, I got it from her. When I was going through the very stressful moments, particularly in the second set when I needed a little bit of a push, I guess she gave me a smile, a fist pump." Novak added that, when he became a father, one of his strongest wishes was that, before he retired from the sport, his children would reach an age where they might witness him winning a Grand Slam, and understand the significance of the situation. After his US Open triumph, he said he was "super blessed" to finally have this wish come true.

One of Novak's many strengths is the way he has continually adapted his training and match play as his career has progressed. Not only does this allow him to counter-punch against the younger players threatening his crown, but it means opponents find it tricky to get the measure of his game. "You need to reinvent yourself because everyone else does," he says, admitting he might be considered a perfectionist. "As a 36-year-old competing with 20-year-olds, I probably have to do it more than I have ever done it in order to keep my body in shape; in order to be able to recover so that I can perform on the highest level consistently. Also, mentally and emotionally [I must] keep the right balance so that I'm actually inspired and motivated to play the best tennis and to compete with these guys – and at the same time keep the playfulness and passion for the sport."

Looking back on his upbringing, in a "family with no tennis tradition", in a "war-torn country going through sanctions and embargo", in a sport that was "unaffordable, unaccessible", he stressed how he had overcome the toughest of odds to reach his current elevated position. "We did it. I say 'we' because I owe a lot to my family; to my parents who sacrificed so much for me to be here. And that's not a cliché. I really mean it. It was extremely, extremely difficult with lots of adversities and atrocities that they had to face – when the last thing you want to think about is supporting your child in an expensive sport. It was more about bringing the bread to the kitchen table, at that point. So reflecting on the whole journey, it's been an incredible, incredible ride that we all can be very proud of."

And in case you worry 24 Grand Slams might have dented his motivation somewhat, then bear this in mind. After his triumph, he said: "I don't want to leave this sport if I'm still at the top; if I'm still playing the way I'm playing."

He insisted he would continue to prioritise the Grand Slams over other tournaments, just as he has done in the past few years. He even joked that he had decades of competitive play left in him: "Eventually one day I will leave tennis: in about 23, 24 years." But then, more realistically, he added: "I don't know how many more seasons I have in my legs."

Fans of this great champion know very well that the legs on this 36-year-old are one of his greatest weapons. No doubt there is hope they hold out so Novak can continue at the top of his game and battle on for more glorious and historic victories.

INDEX

Number italics are pages with captions.

SELECT BIBLIOGRAPHY

ONLINE:

- *Novak Djokovic: The Biography* by Chris Bowers (John Blake Publishing, 2014)
- *Serve to Win: The 14-day Gluten-free Plan for Physical and Mental Excellence* by Novak Djokovic (Bantam Press, 2013)
- *Newsweek* magazine
- *Men's Health* magazine
- *Forbes* magazine
- *The Drinks Business* magazine
- *Vino & Fino* magazine
- *Gulf News* newspaper
- *Shortlist* magazine
- *The New York Times* newspaper
- *The Guardian* newspaper

ONLINE:

- In Depth with Graham Bensinger (podcast)
- London Real (podcast and YouTube channel)
- BBC.co.uk
- Realtor.com
- Leadersmag.com
- TennisMajors.com
- ATPtour.com

PICTURE CREDITS

6-7 Tim Clayton-Corbis/Contributor/Getty; 8-9 Chris Trotman/Stringer/Getty; 10-11 Lionel Cironneau/Associated Press/Alamy Stock Photo; 12-13 Vladimir Zivojinovic/Stringer/Getty; 15 ANNE GUARDIOLA/DPPI Media/Alamy Stock Photo; 16 MIKE NELSON/AFP/Contributor/Getty; 17 E.D. Torial/Alamy Stock Photo; 19 Marija Krcadinac/Shutterstock; 20-1 Andy Cheung/Contributor/Getty; 23T Armando Franca/Associated Press/Alamy Stock Photo; 23B Leo Mason/Popperfoto/Contributor/Getty; 24T PA Images/Alamy Stock Photo; 24B Emmanuel Wong/Stringer/Getty; 27 Cynthia Lum/WireImage/Contributor/Getty; 28 Nikola Krstic/Alamy Stock Photo; 30 Julian Finney/Staff/Getty; 33 TOUSSAINT KLUITERS/AFP/Staff/Getty; 34-5 Julian Finney/Staff/Getty; 36-7 Vladimir Zivojinovic/Stringer/Getty; 38-9 Vesnaandjic/Getty; 40 TORSTEN BLACKWOOD/AFP/Staff/Getty; 41 Jim Spellman/WireImage/Contributor/Getty; 42-3 ALEXA STANKOVIC/AFP/Stringer/Getty; 44 Julian Finney/Staff/Getty; 45T ANDREJ ISAKOVIC/AFP/Stringer/Getty; 45B Julian Finney/Staff/Getty; 46-7 ANDREJ ISAKOVIC/AFP/Stringer/Getty; 48 Julian Finney/Staff/Getty; 49L PEDJA MILOSAVLJEVIC/AFP/Contributor/Getty; 49R PEDJA MILOSAVLJEVIC/AFP/Contributor/Getty; 50-1 BEHROUZ MEHRI/AFP/Contributor/Getty; 52T ANDREJ ISAKOVIC/AFP/Contributor/Getty; 52B Srdjan Stevanovic/Stringer/Getty; 55 Ezra Shaw/Staff/Getty; 56 Clive Brunskill/Staff/Getty; 57 PA Images/Alamy Stock Photo; 58-9 PCN Photography/Alamy Stock Photo; 60-1 AELTC/Bob Martin/Pool/Getty; 62 JACK GUEZ/AFP/Contributor/Getty; 63L Al Bello/Staff/Getty 63R Frank Molter/Alamy Live News; 64 Quality Sport Images/Contributor/Getty; 65 Andrej Cukic/Associated Press/Alamy Stock Photo; 66 Gary M Prior/Allsport/Staff/Getty; 67T Ed Lacey/Popperfoto/Contributor/Getty; 67B FABRICE COFFRINI/AFP/Staff/Getty; 68T ANDREJ ISAKOVIC/AFP/Stringer/Getty; 69T PA Images/Alamy Stock Photo; 70 Bai Xue/Xinhua/Alamy Live News; 74 ANDREJ ISAKOVIC/AFP/Stringer/Getty; 75 Julian Finney/Staff/Getty; 76-7 DIMITAR DILKOFF/AFP/Staff/Getty; 79 Julian Finney/Staff/Getty; 80-1 Clive Brunskill/Staff/Getty; 82-3 Srdjan Stevanovic/Staff/Getty; 84T Arturo Holmes/ATP Tour/Contributor/Getty; 84B Simon Bruty/Any Chance/Contributor/Getty; 85 JOE KLAMAR/AFP/Staff/Getty 86 Victor Joly/Alamy Stock Photo; 88 Julian Finney/Staff/Getty; 89 Clive Brunskill/Staff/Getty; 90 Clive Brunskill/Staff/Getty; 91T Stephen Dunn/Staff/Getty; 91B Sanjin Strukic/Pixsell/MB Media/Contributor/Getty; 93 Leon Neal/Staff/Getty; 94 Andy Cheung/Contributor/Getty; 95 Julian Finney/Staff/Getty; 96 Manny Hernandez/Contributor/Getty; 99 Clive Brunskill/Staff/Getty; 100-1 Julian Finney/Staff/Getty; 102-3 Julian Finney/Staff/Getty; 104-5 Charles Eshelman/Contributor/Getty; 106 DIMITAR DILKOFF/AFP/Staff/Getty; 107 Felipe Dana/Associated Press/Alamy Stock Photo; 110 Michael Steele/Staff/Getty; 111L Karwai Tang/WireImage/Contributor/Getty; 111R Charlotte Wilson/Offside/Contributor/Getty; 114 Dimitrios Kambouris/Staff/Getty; 115 Michael Heiman/Staff/Getty; 116 Bertrand Rindoff Petroff/French Select/Contributor/Getty; 119 Justin Setterfield/Staff/Getty; 120-1 PA Images/Alamy Stock Photo; 123 Nick Laham/Staff/Getty; 124TL Clive Brunskill/Staff/Getty; 124TR Clive Brunskill/Staff/Getty; 124B Al Bello/Staff/Getty; 126-7 Patrick McDermott/Stringer/Getty; 128-9 Mark Brown/Contributor/Getty; 130-1 Grace Chiu/UPI/Alamy Stock Photo; 132T Mark Brown/Contributor/Getty; 132B Mike Coppola/Staff/Getty; 133T Dave M. Benett/Contributor/Getty ; 133B Mark Brown/Contributor/Getty; 136-7 Ibrahim Ezzat/NurPhoto/Contributor/Getty; 138 Vladimir Zivojinovic/Stringer/Getty; 141 Srdjan Stevanovic/Stringer/Getty; 143 Theo Karanikos/Associated Press/Alamy Stock Photo; 144TL Aaron Favila/Associated Press/Alamy Stock Photo; 144TR WENN Rights Ltd/Alamy Stock Photo; 144B Aaron Favila/Associated Press/Alamy Stock Photo; 145 PA Images/Alamy Stock Photo; 146-7 Cameron Spencer/Staff/Getty; 148-9 Rob Carr/Staff/Getty; 150-1 Clive Mason/Staff/Getty; 152 Mark Baker/Associated Press/Alamy Stock Photo; 155 ETIENNE TORBEY/AFP/Contributor/Getty; 156 WENN Rights Ltd/Alamy Stock Photo; 160 Adam Pretty/Staff/Getty; 163 THOMAS SAMSON/AFP/Stringer/Getty; 164 Aurelien Meunier/Contributor/Getty; 165 Clive Brunskill/Staff/Getty; 166T Rindoff Petroff/Hekimian/Contributor/Getty; P166B Bettmann/Contributor/Getty; 167 PHILIPPE LOPEZ/AFP/Staff/Getty; 168-9 Dennis Grombkowski/Staff/Getty; 170-1 Aaron Favila/Associated Press/Alamy Stock Photo; 172-3 Johnny Fidelin/Icon Sport/Contributor/Getty; 174-5 ANDREJ ISAKOVIC/AFP/Contributor/Getty; 176 Srdjan Stevanovic/Stringer/Getty; 177 Associated Press/Alamy Stock Photo; 178 STR/AFPTV/AFP/Contributor/Getty; 181 Elsa/Staff/Getty; 183 Frank Molter/Alamy Stock Photo; 184-5 Dita Alangkara/Associated Press/Alamy Stock Photo; 187 Clive Brunskill/Staff/Getty; 188-9 Clive Brunskill/Staff/Getty; 190 Julian Finney/Staff/Getty; 191T Julian Finney/Staff/Getty; 191B Julian Finney/Staff/Getty; 192-3 Julian Finney/Staff/Getty; 194-5 Frank Molter/dpa picture alliance/Alamy Live News; 196-7 Srdjan Stevanovic/Contributor/Getty; 198 PASCAL GUYOT/AFP/Staff/Getty; 200-1 Maddie Meyer/Staff/Getty; 202 Clive Brunskill/Staff/Getty; 204 STR/AFP/Stringer/Getty; 207 DANIEL LEAL/AFP/Contributor/Getty; 208-9 Ben Queenborough/Alamy Stock Photo; 210 SEBASTIEN BOZON/AFP/Contributor/Getty; 211 Simon M Bruty/Anychance/Contributor/Getty; 212TL Clive Brunskill/Staff/Getty; 212TR Ryan Pierse/Staff/Getty; 212B Clive Brunskill/Staff/Getty; 213 Julian Finney/Staff/Getty; 214-5 Tnani Badreddine/DeFodi Images/Contributor/Getty; 216-7 Action Plus Sports Images/Alamy Live News; 218 Karwai Tang/WireImage/Contributor/Getty; 219L Clive Brunskill/Staff/Getty; P219R Fox Photos/Hulton Archive/Stringer/Getty; 220 Tim Clayton - Corbis/Contributor/Getty; 221 BRENTON EDWARDS/AFP/Contributor/Getty; 222 Tim Clayton - Corbis/Contributor/Getty; 225 GABRIEL BOUYS/AFP/Contributor/Getty; 227 Asanka Brendon Ratnayake/Associated Press/Alamy Stock Photo; 228T Newscom/Alamy Live News; 228B Frank Molter/Alamy Live News; 229 Asanka Brendon Ratnayake/Associated Press/Alamy Stock Photo; 230-1 Quinn Rooney/Staff/Getty; 232 Tim Clayton-Corbis/Contributor/Getty; 234 Matthew Stockman/Staff/Getty

Graphics created by Dave Jones